MOURNING THE LIVING

When the Loved One You've Lost is Still Here

∞

MELODY MURRAY MA, LMFT, CMHS

Edited by Catherine Yarborough

Book Design by - DreamEmpire Publishing

Cover Art by - Joyce Licorish – DreamEmpire Publishing
and Josh Horvath

Paperback 979-8-9876367-8-7

Hardcover 979-8-9876367-7-0

Printed in the United States of America

First Printing Edition, Fall 2023

PUBLISHING

For author booking inquiries, contact:
DreamEmpire Publishing
3775 Venture Drive A-202, Duluth, GA 30096
(678)539-0997 | www.DreamEmpirePublishing.com

i

DEDICATION

This book is dedicated to my grandparents: Amos and Cecile May of Alvin, Texas. They were pillars of a community that loved and respected them. Without them, I would not be who I am. And, I like who I am A LOT.

Friends, family, strangers - we all have an impact on each other. Our choice is whether or not that impact is positive or negative.

Big love to my first teachers in my mental health career:

Therapists: John Foster Elliott, Susan "Nikki" Golden, Ann Worley, Dr. Phaizon Wood, Samantha Oppenheimer, Suzan Scudder, Gazelle Williams, Elizabeth Goodman.

Family and Friends: Annie Belle May, Catherine Yarborough, Camille Murray, Cecily Messer, Grant Pesak, Anthony Jackson, Jake Parks, Teresa Hsu, Evelynn Graham, Alicia Keating, Tiffany Fordham, Chad Caldwell, Erica Niemi and Meg Coon.

Special Thanks to my guardian angel - Martha Stanville and personal cheerleaders - Wendy Miller and Tammi Leader Fuller.

DISCLAIMER

The author and the publisher disclaim any liability arising directly or indirectly from the use of this book. The author will not accept any responsibility for any omissions, misinterpretations, or misstatements that may exist within this book. The author is not engaged in rendering medical services. This book should not be construed as medical advice, nor should it take the place of consistent engagement with a healthcare professional. No warranty, expressed or implied, is delivered by the author or publisher with respect to the contents of this work.

PREFACE

I've always been one of those people that absolute strangers spill their guts to. People say I make them feel comfortable very quickly and I take so much pride in that. I speak to everyone without judgment while maintaining the same level of respect regardless of age, race, gender, or socioeconomic status. This way of relating has helped me in all aspects of my life. For several years I worked in the entertainment industry, from assisting executives to hosting a children's show, producing, and directing reality tv shows and doing stand-up comedy - I like being on my toes, adrenaline flowing.

As much as I loved the excitement, travel and pay (especially the pay) while working in entertainment, I felt I needed to contribute more to the world. One day while I was driving on the 405 in Los Angeles. I saw a bumper sticker that changed the course of my life forever. It read, "Be what you needed as a child." That moment rocked my world! I needed so many things as a kid - validation, guidance, support, safety and, and, and... I realized that I didn't want the loneliness and fear I felt in my chaotic childhood to be in vain, so I decided to go back to school and become a mental health therapist. At that point I'd been in counseling for a few years with an amazing therapist named John Foster Elliott. He helped me process my childhood which led to me loving and accepting myself and my circumstances as an adult. He helped me create and maintain boundaries and shake out anger I didn't realize I even had. He was a steady force, consistent confidante and soft-landing space for me when my life was too much. I'm so grateful for him. I asked for his opinion on me becoming a therapist. I figured, if I'm too crazy to do it, my own therapist would tell me, right? Well, he didn't call 911. He supported my transition from tv producer to graduate student receiving a Master's in Clinical Psychology.

As a Licensed Marriage and Family Therapist, I've worked with children, adults, adolescents, couples and families. I enjoy helping clients rediscover their strengths or discover their strengths for the first time. I like guiding people towards self-love and acceptance while they manage their emotions and behaviors associated with childhood trauma, work stress, depression, anxiety, low self-esteem, and relationship issues. In addition to private practice, for several years I conducted mental health evaluations in a hospital emergency department. I also provide therapy in schools for students in crisis due to trauma, substance abuse and domestic violence of their caregivers, food and housing insecurities, bullying, etc. I utilize intensive training in trauma as well as personal experiences to help people become healthy, positive, self-sufficient and confident.

My favorite topic to speak about and teach is Family of Origin (FOO), essentially, our first roommates – our families. They are the first people we live with and teach us how to relate to others. Most of our adult identity is created in the earliest stages of our lives. Their imprints on us start in utero as opposed to previously thought was the infancy stage. Our DNA carries more than hair and eye color. We now know that mental illness, the gender of your children (X and Y chromosomes from your father) and even egg production and viability are inherited. This core group teaches us (positively or negatively) how to communicate and relate to others, take care of ourselves, how or even if we process our experiences, and so much more. Our family of origin is our first teacher on how to navigate and exist in relationships with others. When your FOO is dysfunctional that can set up a ripple of unhealthy relationship patterns and behavioral issues including violence and addiction. Repeatedly dating the wrong people, physically abusing others, emotionally neglecting, or shaming your children, repetitive job terminations or peer disputes, etc. We need to study how our families influence our behavior in order to see what is being repeated.

In the last few years multiple issues have called us to analyze the strength and necessity of certain relationships based on individual responses to myriad topics including racism, the opioid crisis, opinions on policing and politics, LGBTQA+ rights, military occupation, Covid impact and response, the economy, the climate and so much more. More and more people are distancing themselves from those who don't see the world the same way. Family estrangement is at an all-time high.

I realized I was on the fence of many connections in my life and wanted to show my process and the process of my friends and clients in navigating these challenging situations. You may have already noticed that I am not a writer. I am a therapist with a desire to help people feel and do better. Please allow for the loss of necessary commas, run-on sentences and dangling participles and misspelled words. I am a therapist with a desire to help. I refuse to hold back ways to help others due to a fear of poor grammar. These words came from my heart and the hearts and lives of people dear to me.

I asked friends and colleagues to share their experiences with toxic family and friends. I asked how they were able to distance themselves from dysfunction people they love, how they recognized and acknowledged the unhealthy parts of themselves, how they severed ties or shifted their expectations in order to co-exist with people they choose to love. I could not be more humbled and honored by their generosity, curiosity, and vulnerability.

These are their stories...

CONTENTS

"Before you silence yourself to keep the peace, ask yourself, "What is the worst thing that can happen if I use my voice?" Usually the answer is, 'This person may dislike me.' That's it. If you are silencing yourself for this reason, they already don't like you. They only like a fictional version of you. Raise your voice."

- Mira Hadlow

INTRODUCTION

When we have conflict with the people in our lives, we wrestle with all the feelings that come with the purpose and necessity of the relationship. Does it provide happiness, security, fulfillment, ecstasy, love, burden, agitation? Sometimes we have to ponder altering our relationships or completely ending them. Are these options you've ever considered?

Death ends the ability to reconcile transgressions. All the things unsaid and unresolved stay that way. Death is final and grieving our losses is necessary in order to honor the people that make an impact in our lives and validate our experiences. When death occurs, some are relieved to put an end to suffering. Some feel the loss of things left unsaid, invalidated, diminished and dismissed by the wounding party. What if the wounding party is still here? What if they are lying beside you now?

Can you adjust your expectations with a person or situation you cannot leave or change? When we can't, the relationship may need to end which can feel like death if we do it or death if we don't.

When relationships are layered with so much history, they can be challenging to navigate for a variety of reasons including uneven power dynamics, unhealed trauma and fear of being misunderstood. *Mourning The Living* explores the challenge in acknowledging, identifying, managing and accepting the emotions connected to the negative experiences we have had with the people we love but, for one reason or another we cannot coexist in our current states. This is not a book for people who want to stay in denial. We must acknowledge what we feel in order to grieve and heal. *Mourning the Living* is based on analyzing your current reality and that requires honesty. You can and must handle the reality of your relationships. Denial is a bullshit waste of your time.

Human beings are connected because we need each other to survive. Growth, expansion, resources, procreation, safety - all depend on connection with others. At any given time we are in a relationship with everyone around us: neighbors, coworkers, other drivers in traffic, diners at restaurants, etc. Close and healthy relationships cannot persist without mutual respect. So, how do you maintain respectful relationships, set boundaries and easily adjust expectations in order to agree on a path forward that respects each person's needs? If you are shifting expectations with family, the pushback can be surprising, even disappointing if you're alone in your desire for change.

Family estrangement is growing. If you are severing ties with family, the pain can feel insurmountable... but it's not. Dr. Karl Pillemer conducted a national study that found 27% of Americans 18 and older had cut off contact with a family member, most of whom reported that they were upset by such a rift. That translates to at least 67 million people nationally – likely an underestimate, Pillemer said, since some are reluctant to acknowledge the problem. Of the more than 1,300 people Pillemer surveyed, 10% reported being estranged from a parent or child, 8% from a sibling and 9% from extended family members including cousins, aunts and uncles, grandparents, nieces and nephews.

There are myriad reasons to terminate or adjust a relationship dynamic. Some circumstances include shielding yourself from another's destructive life choices (substance abuse, living a life of crime or with dysfunctional partners), differences in political ideologies or sexual proclivities. "Pathways to estrangement vary", Pillemer said, "but often are linked to early experiences with harsh parenting, parental favoritism and parental divorce. Other common triggers of family rifts include tension with in-laws; disputes over money, inheritances and business deals; and value differences and unrealistic expectations. "Each situation", Pillemer said, "involves a breakdown of family bonds, typically coupled with poor and increasingly hostile communication. Long-simmering feuds may culminate in a 'volcanic event' in which one family member declares "I'm done" with another."

Regardless of the reasons, it's hard to draw a line in the sand and say, "No more" or be on the receiving end of a loved one's decision to cut you off. If you are a partner, friend, child, or parent you may need to adjust your expectations in order to withstand circumstances beyond your or a loved one's control. Consider caring for a partner or child with chronic medical issues or severe mental illness. These situations can be considered too much for someone to handle.

When we are assessing our ability to maintain a relationship, we have to consider how the relationship feels. Do you feel used? Secure? Abused? Celebrated? Loved? Trapped? Fulfilled? Ignored? In order to figure out what to do, you need to know how you feel first. Acknowledging feelings is a difficult thing for many people. Mainly, it's dependent on how feelings were handled by the people who raised us. The healthiest foundation is when you are encouraged to explore your emotions and express your feelings in real time in order to gain validation without judgment. You were safe and protected. And when things went wrong you were taught how to deal with disappointment and pain and learn from it. You were praised when things were going well. You were taught empathy and how to view the whole person, not flaws and faults. You were taught how to create and maintain healthy boundaries without feelings of guilt.

Unfortunately, a healthy loving start isn't the case for all of us. Many, myself included, were emotionally neglected very early on in life which taught us to suppress our feelings, put others' needs ahead of our own, engage in self-destructive self-soothing behavior and fear trusting others and sadly, ourselves. Having your feelings suppressed by the adults raising you sends a variety of negative messages. We may feel that our experiences aren't important therefore neither are our feelings about those experiences. Unfortunately, we tend to carry these false opinions into our adult relationships which can present as low self-worth. We can internalize our caregivers' passivity to mean emotions are unnecessary, are bad or only expressed by weak people. For people who have experienced chronic trauma, feeling like you're always in survival mode can be your default setting. Unfortunately acknowledging and addressing emotions is a luxury many think they cannot afford. The vulnerability required is too scary. Regardless of the lack of early healthy guidance, we have to acknowledge our emotions and express our feelings to ourselves and the people with whom we relate.

We are taught how to write our names and tie our shoelaces. We must also be taught how to protect ourselves physically, spiritually and emotionally. We need to learn how to create and engage in healthy relationships, effectively express ourselves, have patience, love and respect for others, and most importantly, ourselves. This book will help you analyze the quality of your relationships. It will also help you to stop putting others' needs ahead of your own by setting boundaries with them and yourself. Its goal is to help you take a sincere look into your patterns, keep what works while discarding what no longer serves you. Yes, people can change if they acknowledge their issues and commit to living in a new way.

This book is not a means to bash your family, but it is an instrument that should be used to shine a light on what's been hiding in darkness and denial. It's important to understand and accept that our parents can't do for us what wasn't done for them. Like everything in life, if you weren't taught how to do it, you need to figure out how to teach yourself. We all have the power to positively or negatively influence those around us. Some of us ruminate on how we may have harmed someone else. Some people behave like a bull in a China shop - wrecking everything they touch without remorse. It is important to learn how to manage the feelings that come up due to another person's behavior because our impact on each other cannot be underestimated. Blood relatives notwithstanding, we must be mindful of the people with whom we choose to interact. And, regardless of blood ties, some people are not healthy enough to be in our lives. You need to use a combination of heart and head to make good decisions because using only your emotions (heart) or only logic (head) to make decisions, this leads to rigid, black and white thinking. Utilizing logic and compassion for yourself and others will help you create a safe space for you to coexist. But, what if that doesn't work and you are considering severing ties? Feelings of guilt may come up when we directly or indirectly choose to place distance between ourselves and others.

In this book I'll give brief explanations on a few different reasons why making and breaking bonds can be challenging. I'll discuss attachment styles, dysfunctional family systems, trauma and codependency. I'll give you a brief glimpse into these concepts so you'll have a better understanding of why you may feel stuck in an endless loop of crappy relationships. Dozens and dozens of books have been written on these topics so it's easy to do a deep dive into each one specifically on your own. All of the interventions discussed during the 'Work with Clients' sections can be used regardless of the relationship dynamic,

In Chapter 1 we'll lay the groundwork for making changes by understanding why navigating some relationships is so challenging. I'll discuss how attachment styles, trauma and dysfunctional family systems and codependency can make it difficult to create positive relationship boundaries. In Chapter 2, I discuss the need for self-care in your daily routine in order to strengthen and calm you. In chapters 3 through 9 you'll read stories and get insight into sessions with clients involving different relationship dynamics including fathers, mothers, partners, etc. All of the client names have been changed to protect their privacy. Only some names, in the stories at the beginning of the chapters, have been changed. Chapter 10 shares multiple approaches to healing your relational issues. Chapter 11 is focused on Forgiveness. And the book wraps up with a list of resources, book recommendations and descriptions of various therapeutic modalities. This book has been a labor of love and I hope it eases some of the pain and frustration that comes with navigating relationships with the toxic people in your life.

PART I

CHAPTER 1

Why Is It So Hard to Maintain Relationships and Boundaries?

When I was 16 years old my first boyfriend came to my house with one of his (teen) buddies to hang out. My mother was home and whenever she was around, I always held my breath. I was constantly anxious because she was impulsive, unpredictable and subversive. My sister and I never knew what she was going to do or say. Regardless, whatever she chose would always embarrass and humiliate us. The guys hung out and, as we talked, my mother continually inserted herself into the conversation. My boyfriend's friend was flirting with my mother (which I don't fault him for. He was a typical teen boy foolishly thinking he had a shot with a beautiful older woman). The problem is, she flirted back. Then, he asked her out on a date... and she said yes. I can't say our mother/daughter relationship devolved at that point. We would've had to have a consistent, loving bond to start with before it could devolve, right? What did happen is I added this situation to the stack of evidence I had against her. Early on I had to let go of any expectation of a healthy mother/daughter bond. She wasn't capable of it. I realized that at 8 years old. I wish my older sister was able to do the same.

Throughout my entire life my mother disrespected boundaries and did whatever she wanted, even if that meant hurting her children, parents, sisters and friends in the process. She was always inappropriate and followed no one's rules but her own. Her personal rules changed depending on the situation or person she needed to sway to her advantage. She just couldn't see past her own needs and desires in order to consider others. How do you maintain a safe distance when you live with someone like this? If she was a white man, she could have been a CEO or President.

No, I've never been on Jerry Springer or Dr. Phil but the families at each other's throats on those shows aren't anomalies. Family fights are as old as families and, in western cultures, family estrangements are rising. Biologically, people need people for survival, children are especially vulnerable. Having the desire to be close to others isn't needy, it's biological. Getting into and more importantly, away from toxic connections can be difficult for this and a variety of other reasons. And, we are attracted to the familiar so we tend to gravitate towards energies we know regardless of whether they are toxic or healthy.

"Boundaries don't prevent me from being the best version of myself. Boundaries allow me to be the best version of myself."
- Lysa Terkeurst

Boundaries are created in order to feel safe as you connect with others. A good way to gauge if a relationship or scenario requires boundaries is noticing when, where and with whom you get frustrated. Do you feel empowered enough to say "no"? Are you able to express frustration? Do you fear disappointing people?

Boundaries are necessary in every relationship because we need to respect ourselves and others at the same time. Unfortunately most of us are taught that when we're younger than someone, their needs and wants are superior to our own agency and autonomy. Two of the most toxic dynamics that exist are parent/child and employee/employer. This is changing but not fast enough. We should all be able to feel comfortable speaking our minds and establishing boundaries with everyone regardless of hierarchy.

Establishing boundaries need not be a formal or confrontational process. We create boundaries so often we don't even realize it most of the time. If your co-workers aren't upset when you don't respond to calls or emails before 8am or after 5pm - They know you have a boundary about doing work during your personal time. Meeting a potential romantic partner for a date in a public place instead of your home or theirs is a boundary. Changing the subject when conversations go into territories you're uncomfortable with (money, sex, religion, politics) is setting a boundary.

There are multiple types of boundaries including communication, physical, emotional, intellectual, financial, etc. and within boundary settings there are different levels including porous, healthy and rigid. All exist so we can feel safe as we interact with others. If someone attempts to create boundaries in their relationship with you it means at least two things:

1. They want to co-exist and make sure <u>you both</u> feel comfortable.
2. They have respect for themselves and value peace in their own lives.

Boundaries also help by protecting your personal resources. You can support someone and put limits on what that means for both parties. And, I highly suggest it. A helpful phrase that demonstrates this is, 'I will care for you but I will not carry you'. It's important to ensure both parties are on the same page. Individually, we have different ideas of what everything means so, if you decide to help someone it's important to discuss in detail what that means for each of you. For example, you have been asked for financial support. Make sure you discuss the amount, if repayment is expected, when and how much (interest) or alternatives to monetary reimbursement. Devotion without boundaries is self-destruction. Although I do believe families should always support each other there are times when one person's passion is another's person's pain.

Boundaries are necessary in every single relationship, especially the relationships with family. Sometimes people think boundaries are created to keep people out of your life. I disagree. We establish boundaries in order to keep people in our lives in a way that we both feel respected. Here are some boundaries you may want to consider incorporating in your relationships.

Physical - Your body and your personal space are included here. How close are you willing to sit to a stranger on the bus, co-worker or on a first date. Are you comfortable with hugs, handshakes or waves? Sex and/or kissing on a first date? You get to decide how and if you want to be touched and by whom. Just make sure you communicate your comfort level. If you want to spend time with family but you know a little exposure goes a long way, consider staying in a hotel rather than your childhood bedroom. Sitting across the room from your critical mother instead of directly beside her. Bring your own vegan dishes instead of getting butthurt that the host didn't make food you like.

Emotional - How much do you express about your personal needs, emotional triggers, wants, fears and desires? What can others expect from you? How do you show love? How do you need to experience love and validation? When are you available to help others and when do you take time for yourself? All are very important questions to ask yourself in relation to others to avoid feeling aggressive, depleted, ignored or a martyr.

Spiritual - Are you open to spiritual or religious conversations? If not, you don't have to explain this to anyone. If so, what kinds of conversations are you willing to have? Holidays, churches, songs, past lives, Christianity only? You get to decide if you're open to hearing about spiritually. Just make sure you express your comfort level as soon as you can.

Financial - Will you be a financial resource for others in need? If not, you don't have to apologize for your decision. If giving is important to you, create a boundary with yourself first. Who will you give it to? Charities? Friends? Family? The Salvation Army Christmas bucket? How much will you give? Loans or gifts? If you are loaning money, when and how do you expect to be repaid? Make sure you communicate all of this information before money exchanges hands.

Time - Time is perishable. Until someone creates a time machine we're stuck with just 24 hours each day. You need to decide how and with whom you spend your time. Who is worth your time? Learning to say no to events can be very empowering. But feeling guilty is a struggle for some. Even if you agree to something, then change your mind, it's okay. I think establishing time boundaries is especially helpful when you have to share space with difficult people. Before engaging, decide how much time you'll dedicate to anything. If you have a family holiday dinner or to attend. You can decide 1. Whether or not you'll participate. 2. What time limits you'll place on your attendance (2 hours maximum, 2 days only). Create your own schedule by being honest about your limits.

Intellectual - How much do you want to share about your personal beliefs? When do you feel comfortable sharing and hearing opposing ideas? Are you only interested in dating people with advanced degrees? Is talking politically a no no? What behavior by others makes you feel dismissed or disrespected? How you choose to communicate with others is also included. I had a coworker who called everyone "bitch" as a term of endearment. I'm a laid-back person who jokes a lot but the word bitch cannot be casually used about me. I told her not to use the word. And, most importantly, I didn't give her an explanation why - that's my personal information. My decision is enough.

Setting boundaries with people who respect you looks very different than setting boundaries with strangers or those with a history of disrespecting you. When setting boundaries with someone who loves or respects you, there's room for negotiation. They are allowed to have input in the boundary, so they feel respected too. They should be allowed to express their feelings about your decision. The more respectful the relationship is, the more flexible you are allowed to be. If you're trying to set a boundary with someone who has repeatedly broken trust, harmed or abused you, there is no room for negotiation. Your boundary is your boundary. Protect yourself. The boundary is a consequence of their behavior, so, you don't need to give a list of explanations or reasons why you're setting it.

You have the right to draw a line in the sand when someone violates your expressed boundaries. "Expressed" is the key here. You cannot expect someone to read your mind and know what you want or don't want. You must be direct and honest as you articulate your needs. Because, believe it or not, ending a relationship is usually connected to you establishing a new relationship with yourself. You've grown and evolved but the people around you haven't. You want to find a new way to interact but the other person doesn't want to make room for the new you which presents a dilemma. Unfortunately, sometimes the healthiest yet hardest decision is to walk away. The desire to "stick it out" comes naturally for some because we don't want to give up. It is very hard to admit something isn't working and we tend to try to find a solution. We also want to experience as little pain as possible so sometimes it feels easier to just put your needs aside and just let it go.

As Glennon Doyle, author of "Untamed" says, "If you have to choose between disappointing yourself or someone else - disappoint them." They'll either get over it or they won't - It's not up to you. Release yourself from feeling responsible for other adults' emotional reactions to... ANYTHING. It's up to each of us to learn healthy ways to respond to the difficulties of life. If you know a 50 y.o. person that screams, cries or insults others when they don't get what they want, it's not your job to mature this person out of their toddler stage of coping. That's their job. Your job is to create boundaries to protect yourself from that person's behavior.

For far too long women have been saddled with the responsibility of serving and protecting nearly everyone around them, except themselves. I urge you to create a boundary with yourself - Speak your mind, trust yourself and make big decisions that serve you without hesitation. You don't need to tiptoe around another adult's potential immature emotional reactions.

It is extremely important to understand that setting and changing boundaries will have repercussions. There are many relationships that exist because you have had no boundaries. Not having boundaries have made you very attractive to some people. Their selfish behavior can run amuck around you and that serves the other person. You are always the designated driver, you pay everyone else's late rent or mortgage, you bail them out of jail, you supply money for their drugs, providing unpaid childcare – You ignore their bad behavior which serves them, not you. So, when you start setting or changing boundaries some of your relationships will end. Good, because they never served you and people need to be responsible for their own behavior. You have not done anything wrong even though these types of people will try to convince you that you have because they have been inconvenienced. If protecting yourself offends someone else, you need to seriously consider ending this relationship. It's one-sided. Don't fear, ending the relationship may not involve a big confrontation or conversation, but sometimes it will. People who don't get what they want from you tend to leave in a huff or simply fade away because you no longer serve them. To some, this will be a heart-wrenching revelation because you were in denial of your actual importance but, it is necessary. You need to see if and how you are valued, and sometimes that means acknowledging you never were valued.

Attachment

In recent years, Attachment Theory has become a very hot topic outside of the usual psychology circles. Attachment Theory was originated by psychiatrist John Bowlby in the 1920s. Bowlby researched the bonds between infants and their primary caregivers and theorized that people are born predisposed with a desire to attach to other humans. Attachment defines the connectedness between people. Ultimately, healthy early attachment means a constant feeling of safety, connection and security. The lack of healthy early attachment can bring about devastating effects on your cognitive, social and emotional well-being. If dysfunctional attachments are not acknowledged and addressed, the ripple effect will be seen in all of your relationships with the most important effect on your children and your children's children. Bowlby identified the following four attachment styles:

I. Secure

II. Anxious-Insecure

III. Avoidant

Attachment Theory was expanded by developmental psychologist Mary Ainsworth in the 1960s and 70s. Dr. Ainsworth researched the impact of maternal nurturing and deprivation to explain the importance of our early bonds within relationships. It's easy to do a deep dive into attachment theory and further research is encouraged. For the sake of brevity, I'll give an abbreviated explanation by referencing a study by Dr. Ainsworth. In 1965 she designed the Strange Situation Procedure observing infant children when they encounter distress connected to the presence and absence of their primary caregiver, which in that era was usually their mothers. The most salient information gathered was observing the infant's response to its mother's exit, return and the introduction of a stranger to the room. Infants were utilized because even at 6 months, babies are able to assess their environment for safety. (It must be said that these categories were created with a Western lens and do not reflect child-rearing techniques and systems in other cultures. For example, in most African cultures, all members of the community raise the children. This means kids have multiple supports that help form personal identity, self-esteem and secure attachments.)

Here is the Research Setup:

A baby (aged 12 – 18 months) is observed as she interacts with her mother, her mother's absence, eventual return and the introduction of a stranger in an unfamiliar environment. The baby's reaction implies the bond between mother and child.

Scenario 1: Baby feels comfortable exploring the room. Mother exits the room. The baby starts crying because she's distressed. When a stranger is introduced to the room, the baby avoids him until mother returns. When the mother returns the tears stop, the baby is relieved with their reunion and she quickly returns to play. Baby girl remembers mom AL-WAYS returns and always attends to her needs. The child feels comfortable exploring and interacting with the stranger when mom is present. The baby knows she is loved and always has a safe person to return to when afraid. This baby has a Secure Attachment.

Scenario 2: Mother exits the room, and her baby starts crying, more intensely than the baby in Scenario 1. When the stranger enters the room, the baby girl shows fear and actively avoids him. When mom returns, instead of relief, the baby is agitated and ambivalent. Baby is so agitated that she resists reuniting and may push mom away or even hit her out of anger for disappointing her again. Mom has been unreliable in her care and love for baby and baby is frustrated with the inconsistency. She cries more and explores less than the babies in the other scenarios. This child has an Anxious/Insecure Attachment.

Scenario 3: Mother and baby enter and play. Mom exits and the baby doesn't flinch. Baby is content to entertain herself and the baby's exploration is the same whether her caretaker is available or not. Baby appears comfortable interacting with the stranger and can even be comforted by him. When mom returns, the baby barely notices. She learned very early that her mother wouldn't satisfy her. Her mother is physically present but not emotionally available. This child has an Avoidant Attachment.

Attachment research did not stop there. Years later, a fourth attachment style called Disorganized Attachment was introduced by Mary Main, a colleague of Dr. Ainsworth's. Children who have experienced violence, chaos or worse – neglect, tend to have disorganized attachment due to their parents' unresolved traumas. Kids have a difficult time understanding how to connect with someone who takes care of them but also causes them harm. Who wouldn't? They have difficulty regulating their emotions which can lead to violent physical and/or verbal outbursts and aggression. Many children who have lived in the foster care system have a Disorganized - Disoriented Attachment. Attachment figures are unreliable and can be scary. We learn to rely on ourselves only and dismiss the need for connection.

People with anxious attachment styles tend to hold onto situations and people longer than is healthy. They find themselves constantly worrying about and wondering where they stand in relationships. They question their own judgment, second-guess their decisions, and tend to allow their emotional state to be in charge. They didn't feel safe exploring their world and personal abilities. We create more insecure strategies to attach to others. People with secure attachment styles usually have high self-esteem and self-worth. They will usually avoid disastrous relationships with unhealthy people due to the ability to set clear boundaries upfront. Adults with disorganized - disoriented attachments will find it difficult to engage in healthy relationships which require vulnerability. Vulnerability requires trust. If you were unable to trust your early caregivers who were supposed to love, guide and protect you, what are the chances you'll feel comfortable trusting and bonding with strangers?

Understanding the ways, you attach will ease your ability to navigate all your relationships, romantic or otherwise. It will also explain why disconnecting from others is effortless or challenging. The good news is that most people have a Secure Attachment Style and it's important to stress that attachment styles are not etched in stone. With therapy and/or patience from a secure partner, friends and/or supportive family, in time you can shift your attachment style from anxious, avoidant, or disorganized to secure.

Attachment wounds occur when there's devastation between people in an intimate relationship no matter whether it's familial, friendship or romantic. You'll know you've experienced an attachment wound when your view of the person drastically changes and your ability to respect them or feel safe with them is shaken. Trust breaches are the most common avenue for these situations but you can repair them in yourself. You need to repair attachment wounds, or you will repeat the pattern of connecting with people who won't give you what you need. Just like all injuries you need time to heal. If you don't heal, you run the risk of repeating this cycle and being reinjured in subsequent relationships.

"Life is a balance of holding on and letting go"
- Rumi

It's natural for people to want to hold onto and fight for a person or situation but, if you notice you are compromising your needs, safety, identity, and desires, you may need to reconsider the relationship. Fear of change, choosing to stay with 'the devil you know rather than the devil you don't', etc., letting go is difficult for many reasons but, also necessary for many reasons. Attachment disruptions lead to struggles with relationship satisfaction, commitment challenges including committing either too soon or not at all.

Attachment theory is not about parent blaming but it is about parental analysis. Looking back on how you were raised helps you understand decisions you've made and can help you learn how to move forward in all of your relationships in healthier ways. Attachment ruptures happen in a variety of ways beyond a parents' control: war resulting in family separations, financial insecurity leading to home loss, parental health issues and hospitalization, substance abuse, death, incarceration and more.

Realizing you have an unhealthy attachment can be very difficult to accept. When you realize someone, you love may be using you - it can feel like a punch in the gut. Are you supposed to treat the person the same way or just suck it up? Do you confront and potentially cause family drama? Do you end the relationship completely and fear getting close to others in the future? You get to decide. I hope you choose you.

Dysfunctional Family Systems

A family system consists of everyone who takes part in raising you, blood-related or not. Your parents, grandparents, siblings, aunts and uncles, foster parents are also in your family system and can be called your family of origin (FOO). Depending on your particular circumstances, all the following people can be a part of your family system as well: Neighbors, stepparents, teachers, preachers, coaches and so on. Your family system includes all of the people who have an influence on how you see yourself and how you react and respond to the world.

There are enmeshed families and differentiated families. Enmeshed families take part in "groupthink" which means the family system, typically led by a patriarch or matriarch, sets the tone for the way the family does everything - educationally, religiously, politically, financially, romantically. Boundaries are vague or nonexistent. Roles are confusing. The house functions according to one person's whim. Have you ever witnessed parents asking their most difficult child to make a choice for the family vacation? See parents ask their kids for advice or money? One parent aligns with a child against the other parent.

An enmeshed parent can be hostile, possessive, highly emotional, intrusive, controlling or competitive towards their children. Enmeshed kids are taught to suppress their emotions and needs in favor of the matriarch or patriarch. They are usually manipulated into feeling guilty for wanting to do their own thing. Some are threatened with abandonment for breaking from family tradition. This is a system where individuality is highly discouraged and often bullied. Enmeshed systems can cause a child to internalize others' behaviors and feel responsible for the emotions of the adults around them.

The healthy and ideal version of a family system is differentiation. The goal of differentiation is to encourage everyone to develop themselves individually while still being supported by and connected to their family. The family welcomes creativity and stimulates engagement with people from different backgrounds, ways of living and loving. Accomplishing personal goals is celebrated. Recognizing, expressing, and being attuned to your own emotional experiences is taught and encouraged. A differentiated person can connect with others while maintaining healthy boundaries and not take on other's issues as their own.

Symptoms of dysfunctional families:

1. Submission is required. Individual thought is discouraged.
2. Being vulnerable is dangerous. Your past is used to hurt you.
3. You must take sides. Grudges are common.
4. Feelings must be suppressed, or you're considered weak.
5. Public image is more important than authenticity and sincerity.
6. Acceptance is conditional and support is transactional.

7. Extreme reactions are normalized.
8. Emotional and psychological abuse are common.
9. Abuse is denied or downplayed.

Unfortunately going to therapy or exploring past traumas are still considered taboo for many people. Often, I hear, "you can't change the past so what's the point of talking about it". The point is shame can be abolished when you realize certain events occurred at no fault of your own. It can be extremely helpful to do a dive into the backgrounds of the people who raised you and have been abusive and disappointed you. Looking into the past can help uncover behavior and unhelpful communication patterns that did not begin with you. So, if you don't like the way you were parented you had better do a deep dive into how that has affected you and make sure you address those things before you have kids of your own. What we don't heal we repeat. We are not necessarily destined to become our toxic parents, but we risk repeating the same negative patterns if dysfunctional parenting behaviors aren't confronted, dismantled and replaced with healthy parenting skills.

Family estrangements are becoming more and more common and 'losing touch' with friends isn't always a passive act. Sometimes we silently walk away because we don't know how to set boundaries or respectfully disagree with someone we really care about. Also, toxic relationships aren't just for lovers. In this book you'll read many stories of toxic relationships with parents, siblings and ourselves.

If any of these situations sound familiar, you are probably in a toxic relationship.

- You're expected to host every social gathering including location, food, clean up, etc.
- You're expected to shoulder the responsibilities for aging parents despite having siblings.

- You're always the designated driver amongst friends and co-workers.
- You're always expected to pay the tab because you're the most financially successful in the group.

Bottom line - If you or your needs are never a priority to certain people in your life you may want to analyze whether the relationship is worth your time.

A special shout out to all who have been groomed to be selfless and give every drop of yourself to others and always putting yourself on the back burner. News Flash: You DON'T owe anyone all of you - not your parents, husband, children, friends or boss. Dismantle the thoughts connected to 'blood is thicker than water' and complete subservience to the people around you equals love. You are not less than anyone. You matter. Your needs, your dreams, your life matters.

We learn what to do, and what not to do from the people around us. They teach us how to brush our teeth, tie our shoelaces and how to hold a fork. I don't know why people stop teaching there without diving into the nuts and bolts of building healthy relationships, how to give and receive love, effective communication skills and emotional health? Families also need to teach compassion, patience, how to identify, articulate, express and process emotions in healthy ways. If you don't know how to teach this to your children, try family therapy to have the therapist teach you. Don't ignore the emotional side of things because you feel ill-equipped. Get equipped and break dysfunctional family patterns.

Trauma

The Pollyanna in me would like to think there are people that have never experienced any kind of trauma but I don't know any of those mythical beings. There are many people who don't think they have experienced trauma. I think this happens for multiple reasons but mainly it is due to them not knowing what trauma is.

Trauma is the act of experiencing a distressing event. Distress means different things to different people, but it usually includes feeling as though your life or livelihood has been threatened. There are different degrees of trauma and how we handle it depends on many factors including age, cognitive development, culture and coping mechanisms.

Trauma is not the same for everyone and many people experience trauma without even knowing it. An event one person feels is traumatic and damaging may not be noticed but someone else and our maturity, coping ability and grounded-ness determines our reaction or response.

Being within an enmeshed community, where everyone around you is doing the same abusive things, will have you thinking you haven't experienced trauma. Being isolated due to geography and religion can have you feeling like your abuse is normal because it is all you know.

Trauma can change everything in our lives including how we see ourselves, how safe or unsafe we see others and the world as a whole. Some experience a shift in their personal identity which will inevitably affect how they function in relationships.

It's important not to dismiss someone else's response to events that you don't personally feel is traumatic. An event that I would perceive as traumatic may not be seen that way for you and vice versa. Judging or diminishing someone's reaction or response to their own experiences can feel dismissive, shaming and disrespectful especially to children. Trauma experienced in childhood changes our brains. Whether it is something that happened to your physical body, surviving an accident or natural disaster, or being deprived of a safe environment with a nurturing caretaker, trauma can shift how we see ourselves: victim or victor; survivor or thriver. Not everyone has the strength or resources to 'pull themselves up by the bootstraps' and 'bounce back'. Resilience is not a built-in trait. Resilience comes from processing and healing after trauma - not just the act of experiencing trauma. Stacking up traumatic experiences doesn't make someone resilient unless they're stacking coping skills as well. Healing is a necessary and delicate process that takes courage. Trauma can have us clinging to unhealthy habits and toxic people simply due to proximity and habit. For substance abusers and partners in domestic violence relationships, being isolated and feeling lonely is quite common. If you're hurt and alienated from your inner circle due to your unhealthy behaviors, you may not have access to them when you need a healthy support system. Those trying to break free and get clean may find it hard to leave their toxic partners or friends because they've lost everyone else in their lives.

Sometimes people repeat their childhood traumas without realizing all those unprocessed wounds are still vibrating within and controlling you on a subconscious level. When you realize you've chosen a partner that acts just like your dismissive father or your best friends only care about themselves like your narcissistic mother, you may have recreated your family of origin (FOO). When you are parenting, dating, working or communicating in ways that trigger volatility, sadness or dissatisfaction, processing your past trauma may be what you need due to your past issues dictating your current emotional and behavioral responses. You may cling too long, or you may end relationships too soon without discussing the issues.

Relational Trauma is caused by prolonged or repeated trauma and abuse. When a child grows up in a household where domestic violence, substance, sexual, verbal abuse and emotional neglect, chaos and instability regularly occur, attachments are fractured if not broken completely. These attachment fractures have a lasting effect on a child's self-image, how they learn to give and receive love and how they perceive their value. My heart broke as infants and children were separated from their parents at the Mexico/US border. The indifference the families were shown coupled with the lack of nurturance the kids are living with will have a ripple effect on our respective countries for generations. Imagine the fear the children feel. The inability to trust those around you as a kid makes it difficult to ask for and receive outside support and love, affects the ability to love and engage in healthy relationships throughout a lifetime.

Symptoms of Relational Trauma can include difficulty creating boundaries, self-esteem struggles, difficulty trusting others, substance abuse, anxiety, depression, and other mental health issues. Relational trauma within families is tricky to navigate because when you decide to kick your grandfather to the curb, you may still bump into him at the family reunion, a wedding or at Thanksgiving dinner. Some never stand up for themselves because they don't want to rock the boat by causing waves in the family. Some say, *blood is thicker than water*. I call bullshit. We all know that family can disappoint you more than anyone else because they know your vulnerabilities. They know your mother is an alcoholic. They remember when you got arrested for public intoxication and you lost your new job. Family can hit below the belt with embarrassing shit that stings worse than any stranger could... which is a big reason why it's hard to stand your ground.

Trauma Bonding

Here's my basic definition of Trauma Bonding: You put me through a lot of shit. I'm going to forgive you even though I'm not healed (and you're not sorry). Now, I'll connect with a bunch of people with your same fucked up energy and call it love even though it's seriously dysfunctional.

There's a slippery slope in trauma healing because outside support is helpful and sometimes necessary in order to process and heal. Group Therapy is an extremely powerful modality because it helps normalize experiences and validate your emotions amongst people with similar experiences. Toxicity occurs when a traumatic event becomes part of someone's identity and their way of connecting to others. Staying in victim mode, gaslighting people and using your trauma to manipulate others can hinder healing and cause the adoption of many dysfunctional traits like self-harm, verbal and physical aggression, substance abuse and toxic relationships. I've seen this occur with adolescents quite often, especially in therapeutic settings. Experiencing trauma can shift one into a lonely place of shame, embarrassment and anger. If you meet someone who accepts you, you may be tempted to connect to diminish your loneliness and feel like a regular person again. But, if that person has experienced similar trauma be mindful of their way of connecting. Are they talking about their trauma in order to process it and they are actively working on healing or are they exploiting their trauma as a way to garner sympathy or manipulate for personal gain? Are they bonding with you to perpetuate a cycle of abuse? This is why I think it's important to stay single while healing. You'll change so much, and you don't want to create bonds and/or commitments with people who are attracted to the damaged part of you.

Codependency

"Saying the phrase, 'That ain't got shit to do with me' has been proven to reduce anxiety." Author Unknown

Toxic people don't usually have boundaries therefore they don't respect boundaries. That's the main reason they are toxic. There's an automatic imbalance in a relationship with a toxic person because it's nearly impossible for anyone else (or their needs) to exist in the toxic person's presence. You need to be vocal and firm about how you want to interact with these people because toxic people can't see outside of themselves. They won't pick up hints or infer anything. They aren't attuned to you so they won't see you because they only see their own wants and needs. You can not 'beat around the bush' with a toxic person. You need to be honest, direct and straight between the eyes when communicating.

Relationships with toxic people usually involve an element of codependency. Early experiences of co-dependency focused on how a woman could best support her alcoholic husband. Since then, the definition has moved beyond dysfunctional relationships with addicts to anyone who puts their energy into a toxic relationship dynamic. Basically, a codependent relationship is a love affair with another person's issues. This can include sacrificing yourself for someone else who is chronically ill, the parents of kids with behavioral problems, dealing with addicts, batterers and more. Believe it or not, a codependent person believes their behaviors are helpful coping strategies including: constantly calling or imposing their "help" on someone, offering or loaning money so the addict doesn't have to do something dangerous to get it, accepting any and all behavior or never setting limits or expectations of healthy behavior under the guise of 'love'. Codependent behavior is people pleasing at an intense level. Having a low self-image contributes to the desire to sacrifice all of you in favor of someone else.

Although toxic people tend to ignore boundaries it doesn't mean it's not worth setting them. You set the boundaries in order to give each party a roadmap for communication and the proverbial line in the sand that should not be crossed. Be vocal and explicit about what someone can and cannot do to you. If they cross that line, that will be the evidence you need to make new decisions about your relationship. You can give them another chance to work on the issues or you can choose to move on. It's important to note that allowing someone to cross your boundaries without consequence destroys any respect the toxic person could have for you. They will continue to test you knowing you will eventually cave because you have a history of caving.

The desire for connection with others is biological. People need people PERIOD. Humans can't thrive without other humans. But, when the relationship turns into something harmful and ugly, it's not a positive connection you're experiencing. If you're giving more than you're getting you need to change how you're engaging, mourn the relationship you wanted, adjust your expectations or sever the relationship completely. Severing a relationship doesn't mean love no longer exists or never existed. Sometimes we need to love people from a distance in order to protect ourselves.

Building up that protective shield starts with self-care. Engaging in healthy routine self-care is extremely important when dealing with life. When you're taking care of yourself physically and psychologically the unexpected blows life throws you won't hit as hard. You're healthier and more balanced, which is necessary when dealing with stressful situations. If you don't value yourself or your own peace it's hard to fathom walking away from a toxic person especially if you have nothing else happening in your life. You can also fool yourself or let them fool you into thinking you're the only one who cares or the only person who can help them.

Some people love to be needed and love to be martyrs. They'd like to believe only they can handle situations the right way. Don't be a martyr. They're so annoying playing the victim and hero simultaneously. Each adult is responsible for their own healing. You are not their savior. Clean up your own backyard before diving into someone else's weeds.

A glaring trait of codependent relationships is abandoning yourself while obsessing over someone else. If you've put yourself on the back burner because you feel another person's needs are greater than yours or they have no one else - You're probably in a codependent relationship. If you're allowing someone else's behavior to affect you, therefore you try to control their behavior - you're probably in a codependent relationship. Do you find your friend circle always filled with troubled, needy people? Honey, you are codependent.

Look into the people around you - Who's toxic? It's extremely important that you limit or completely eliminate the number of toxic people in your life, yes, even family members. You need to limit their access to your resources, energy, time and love and accept that you'll never get a reciprocal outpouring of support or love. It is what it is.

CHAPTER 2

Self-Care

My therapeutic relationships always begin with discussions of self-care. When you have decided to change your life and have made the choice to heal, you will need to strengthen yourself spiritually, emotionally and physically in order to get through interactions, conversations, boundary setting or anything that stands between you and your peace.

Self-Care includes any and everything we do to feel good. It's so much more than massages and mani/pedis. Those are great but can be expensive and inconvenient if you don't have money, childcare or time. Self-care should be expanded to include avoiding things or people that increase stress and strife. I don't mean putting your head in the sand to avoid anything uncomfortable. I mean avoiding voluntary interactions that serve others but not yourself. For example, declining the party invite of a toxic relative or frenemy (friend/enemy: someone you dislike but fake closeness). Insisting your high maintenance mother stay in a hotel rather than using your couch, even if you have to pay for it yourself. Buying grocery store cupcakes on the way to school instead of staying up all night baking them for the classroom party your kid forgot to mention. Self-Care is exercising, eating healthy, having sex and walking in nature as well as saying "no" to anything that doesn't serve you.

If you've never experienced sincere love and kindness, it may be difficult for you to take care of yourself. You may not be accustomed to good treatment starting with you instead of being attached to someone outside of you. If your love (or idea of love) always comes from something external you could fall prey to a love-bombing narcissist without knowing their "loving" behavior is false and manipulative. You need to actively experience loving and accepting yourself so you're able to discern what's healthy and positive vs behavior that is negative and toxic. The reason I stress self-care, and especially the non-traditional aspects of it, is because it's important to be loving towards yourself, especially if your work, relationships or health are challenging and don't satisfy your needs.

Self-care is not selfish. I repeat, SELF-CARE IS NOT SELFISH. It's not self-centered or wasteful either. It is a necessity. Feeling rested and balanced gives us the ability to navigate life from a strong, healthy and confident place. In order to have the tough conversations you will need to have you need to adopt, or enhance, your self-care regimen making it a daily practice including healthy eating, journaling, planning for the future, being present and in the moment, exercise, dancing, therapy, sex, quality sleep, creativity and more. You need to have a daily routine that isn't abandoned when you get a new lover, new job or annoying request from your needy sister. You need a routine because you will get stressed out and that's when you will need your routine the most. Self-care doesn't prevent life from happening, but it definitely helps you handle life from a place of stability and calm. Find Self-Care pdfs online and keep tips on your phone and posted around your office and home to make it easy to reach for something healthy to soothe you. You need to take care of yourself every day, all day. Make it a priority.

People who've experienced childhood trauma usually struggle adopting self-care because their needs were not prioritized by their early caregivers. When your personality was formed in an emotionally neglectful environment, you'll accept scraps thinking they are prime cuts because you don't know the difference. Maintaining a self-care routine, understanding attachment styles and healing relational trauma will provide you with a foundation to understand your needs, patterns, motivations, strengths and weaknesses. Thus, you will notice an improvement in the quality of your relationships.

Surprising versions of self-care include removing yourself from stressful situations (jobs and relationships), declining invitations to weddings, showers (baby/bridal/wedding) I find them boring as fuck and major time wasters), kids' birthday parties and even some vacations. I cancelled my own birthday trip to see friends after I announced my separation and impending divorce. (I didn't want to have to answer the same questions over and over again.) How about you NOT answer every phone call, delaying replies to texts or emails? Just saying "no" and choosing to care for yourself instead of over-extending yourself for the sake of someone else. Going to the gym, engaging in creative pursuits (making and listening to music), self-reflection (journaling, attending church, meditating), napping without an alarm clock to wake you... Be patient with you.

Consider creating a Self-Care First Aid Kit. Cherly Richardson, a self-care expert, created a list of questions to ask yourself to help create your kit.

1. Who can I turn to for support when I'm afraid? Who comforts me, makes me feel safe and allows me to have my feelings?

2. Whom do I need to avoid? Who adds to my anxiety level, overwhelms me with questions or has a tough time listening without interrupting me?

3. What does my body need to feel nurtured, strong and healthy?

4. What unhelpful coping strategies or activities do I need to avoid?

5. What do I need to feel comforted at this time?

Cheryl offers so much insight and ideas on ways to take care of yourself.

It's also necessary to identify your values. Who do you want to be and what do you want your life to represent? Values are rarely ever discussed but extremely helpful when you find it difficult to make decisions. Do a google search for 'List of Values' and you'll see multiple lists with dozens of values. Review the list and choose 5-10 values that resonate. A few of my values include: authenticity, adventure, boldness and legacy. Depending on the list you're using you may find terms that overlap like altruism, philanthropy, and social justice. Feel free to combine terms where there are similar goals. Think about why particular terms speak to you and how you'd like them incorporated in your life. It's a simple process that can deliver profound insight. I highly recommend it. When you're having a difficult time making a decision, review your list of values. If the decision is in line with who you are/want to be - go for it. If a decision is not in line with your values... you know what you need to do. When you lack a healthy relationship with yourself and if you don't prioritize your peace, it's very easy to become engaged in unhealthy relationships and even harder to get out of them. All of these changes will make it easier for you to set and maintain boundaries with the people around you and, most importantly, yourself because no one will protect you better than you.

Radical Self-Care

"Love is generally taught to us by our caretakers and be-
comes the foundation of our belief system around love. If
that love is rooted in toxic beliefs and behaviors, as the in-
dividual in a family system begins to heal, limiting conver-
sations or removing them from your life until they learn
to practice a new version of healthy love is a form of radi-
cal self-care." Denise Williams LMFT.
www.Well-Play.com

Radical Self-Care is intense because it encompasses those big, life-changing decisions that will improve your life but, in the process, will shake it up BIGTIME. Radical self-care can include initiating separation or divorce, quitting a high paying/high stress job, moving to a new state or country away from your family of origin. Radical self-care is the act of making your needs a priority above everyone else's needs. You have to put on your mask before you assist others, thus, your emotional safety is your main goal. This is hard for most women thanks to the patriarchy. Men have been prioritizing their needs and putting them in women's laps since the dawning of time. They don't feel guilty about it so why should we?

Yes, you can make these big moves without feeling guilty, but you have to set boundaries with yourself first. You have to be honest about your current level of happiness and your current level of misery. What can be changed? What do you have control over? This is an opportunity to brainstorm what you truly want in life. WRITE IT DOWN! Write down what you want and need. Also take time to think about what has held you back - implied familial responsibilities, expectations, childhood fairytale dreams of a less mature self, shame for making a decision that didn't bring the joy you expected. Listen, if you let outside people determine your relationship, career and family goals then why are you going to let the same people shame you into staying within those miserable situations? Who is your master? Who are you living for?

Staying in a miserable marriage serves no one, especially your children. They can see you're miserable and so can your friends, family and neighbors. Your kids see your passive aggressive behavior towards each other, your fear, disappointment, anger. Staying together when you're miserable is not teaching them commitment, you're teaching them to put their head down and bathe in misery so everyone else is 'comfortable'. No, this marriage and family therapist is not saying everyone should get divorced when life isn't puppies and rainbows. I am saying be honest with yourself about what can be changed and what cannot be compromised.

The stress of staying in a miserable job can literally kill you. Karoshi is the Japanese term for "overwork death". People dying due to strokes and heart attacks connected to the stress of their jobs. There is an entire choir filled with wives of men who died on the job due to stress. There are some cultures where people are being shamed for working less than 16 -18-hour days and being called "lazy" when they go home or on vacation. Our jobs take time away from our families, hobbies and make an impact on our health so you better make sure it's worth it. But, what if it isn't? It usually isn't. Do you want to break free of this cycle but aren't supported in doing so? Take the time to sit and think about it. How can you downsize: A smaller home, paying cash for a car less sexy, less afterschool activities for your children. How much does your job serve your or your partner's ego? Sometimes our stress is in the form of a dysfunctional relationship with our partner, dependent children or ourselves. I knew of a man working in his 77s, afraid to retire because of his lazy adult children who refused to get jobs and financially support themselves. If a relationship only brings you pain, what's the upside of maintaining the relationship?

More on Self-Care While Reading

As you work through this book, listen to your body, mind and spirit. Reading these stories will have you thinking about your relationships. It's supposed to. When you feel the situation becoming intense - listen to yourself and: take a break, drink some water or tea, go on a walk, listen to music, wrap yourself in a blanket, lie down, talk to a friend. No need to power through. Think about the pain you feel if you eat something too fast. Think about brain freeze from eating ice cream... Take your time with this. When necessary, sit the book down and step away. Come back when you're calm, rested, hydrated.

It will also be helpful to note which passages trigger you. It will benefit you to lean into your triggers when you have a self-care routine firmly in place - not before. Make sure you have several healthy coping mechanisms to access when the going gets tough.

PART II

All of the stories at the beginning of Chapters 3 - 9 were solicited in order to normalize estrangement and highlight the difficulty maintaining relationships with people closest to us. These stories are shaded in gray with most, but not all, names disguised with permission from the contributors. The stories were printed as they were submitted with minimal editing for grammar.

CHAPTER 3

Fathers

> *"You gotta understand that some people never really grow up. They never learn their lesson. They never recognize their mistakes; they never acknowledge their faults. They never admit when they are wrong. You will never receive an apology from them, and you will never see their behavior change."*
> *- Author Unknown.*

Being a good father has many expectations: leader, provider, hero, nurturer, protector... We all deserve to have fathers with these healthy traits and more but, as much as we deserve them, we don't always get them. In parenting, the goal cannot be "perfection" or whatever that means. The goal should be providing a consistent and positive connection which helps your kids feel protected, stable and secure. A 2019 research study by Susan Woodhouse found that a parent only has to get it right 50% of the time to be a "good enough" parent. You can still be okay and have a good life having been raised by someone who is just 'good enough'. The problems arise when people fall short and damage their children.

If your father isn't who you hoped he would be, how do you reconcile that? What part of his behavior has been integrated into your identity, behavior in relationships and parenting skills? Don't underestimate this. What of his positive traits do you have and take pride in? Which traits are negative and destructive? This requires self-awareness, honesty and time because healing is necessary especially if you decide to be a parent. I don't think it's inevitable that we turn into our parents, especially when they didn't raise us BUT, when you share DNA, blue eyes may not be the only thing that gets passed down to you.

Like women, men are given mixed messages about who they are supposed to be and contradictory paths on how to get there. Are you the provider or the nurturer? Are you the protector, the affectionate parent or the disciplinarian? What if you want to be all of the above? What if you were taught that being a man meant being tough and emotionless? Some men receive this message and that all that is required of them is providing a paycheck and discipline and that's it. How are you supposed to be a partner and parent with this message as your guide? It is difficult but essential to look at our family members and challenge what they have taught us to be and believe.

Some traditions must be broken when their goal is inappropriate, antiquated, abusive or damaging. Corporal punishment was once ubiquitous. Over the years multiple studies have revealed the damage done when kids are physically assaulted and/or emotionally neglected by their fathers. Using the word "abuse" was once never connected to parenting. It was considered discipline and widely accepted. Ever watch the 60's era hit television show "Mad Men"? In the premiere episode boys are giggling and running through the house then bump into a table. A man slaps one of the boys. Moments later another man arrives, finds out the kids' behavior and also slaps the boy. Eventually the damaging effects of corporal punishment became known and now much of it is illegal and can be investigated through Child Protective Services. Nevertheless, many people were raised this way and continue the practice with their children and grandchildren.

There are many different types of fathers. Yes, there are amazing dads out there but in order for you to heal we're focusing on the ones that caused issues with your identity, self-esteem and healthy attachment to others. In Lindsay C. Gibson's book, "Adult Children of Emotionally Immature Parents" she gives great descriptions of some parents who leave abandoned, confused and angry children in their wake, knowingly or unknowingly. Emotionally immature parents create emotional insecurity in their children. Can you spot yours in the following descriptions?

Emotional Parents are controlled by their feelings vacillating between overinvolvement and abrupt withdrawal. They are prone to instability and unpredictability and rely on others to stabilize them. Small upsets are treated like the end of the world and everyone has to pay for this parent being inconvenienced in any way.

Driven Parents are compulsively goal-oriented and super busy. They can't stop trying to perfect everything, including other people. They rarely pause long enough to have true empathy for their children. They are controlling and can't help interfering in their children's lives.

Passive Parents have a laissez-faire mindset and avoid dealing with anything mildly upsetting. They are less obviously harmful than the other types of parents but their emotional disconnection has damaging effects. They easily defer to a dominant partner which includes allowing abusive behavior to occur. They cope by minimizing problems and acquiescing. You can identify these parents by their admission that their child is their best friend.

Rejecting Parents engage in a range of behaviors that make you wonder why they decided to have children at all. They don't enjoy emotional intimacy and clearly don't want to be bothered by children. They have little or no tolerance for other people's needs. Their actions include blowing up, issuing commands and isolating from other family members. They show little closeness or real engagement. They mostly want to be left alone.

There are a multitude of reasons why people turn out like this. Typically, people repeat what they experienced. Abuse such as emotional neglect, physical and sexual abuse can aid in creating all of these parenting styles. Not all people who grow up with these parents repeat negative parents. And, as one of my graduate school professors stated, "Just because you know why someone is an asshole, that does not give them a right to be an asshole." Being citizens of the world who affect each other, gives you the responsibility to heal yourself.

So, which father do you have? How have you translated his abusive parenting, or lack thereof, into your identity? Here are a few ways (this list will appear in the chapter on Mothers too) being emotionally or physically abandoned by your father can look:

- **Low self-esteem or sense of self:** If the person who created you isn't there for you, then you feel you have no value—difficulty trusting others and yourself.
- **People Pleasing** – Diving into or staying in unhealthy relationships quickly. Doing too much for others or doing things you don't want to do so others won't leave you.
- **Relationship Issues** – Attaching too quickly to the wrong people or not attaching to anyone at all. The eternal bachelor – no one is ever good enough; the loner who sticks to themselves—feeling unworthy of anyone's love or attention. Also, choosing people who will abandon you because they are unavailable to you physically (married, live

far away, entrenched in a job or hobby you can't participate in) – creates a self-fulfilling prophecy.

- **Hypersexuality:** You want love and intimacy, but since
  that wasn't healthily modeled for you, you choose sex to
  be close to others.
- **Toxic Masculinity** – You may have a skewed vision of
  what manhood means, so your version is heightened and
  threatening.
- **Fear of letting go** – It's hard for you to walk away from
  toxic jobs, toxic relationships, status symbols you can't
  afford to maintain.
- **Addictions and addictive behavior:** If you weren't
  taught healthy ways to take care of yourself when
  stressed, you look for ways (usually maladaptive) to
  soothe.
- **Hyperarousal** - Never feeling safe, secure, or settled in
  anything: your identity, your home, your job, or your relationships.
- **Needing Constant Distraction** - You find being alone
  with yourself, your thoughts, and emotions difficult so
  you are always filling time and space with people, errands, activities, your phone, etc.

Suppose you recognize yourself in any of these descriptions and
you want to be in a relationship with other people (friends, partners, roommates, or become a parent). In that case, you need to
heal, or you'll repeat the pain that was inflicted on you but, you'll
be the perpetrator or continual victim.

Trinity's father

I'm third generation born on my father's side so my family came
from Russia and Poland through Ellis Island and landed in
Brooklyn. There's an entire history of the Jewish identity and
lived experience which meant that being an Ashkenazi Jew in
the United States of European ancestry, that allowed entry into

whiteness - in the upper mobility and advancement that meant letting go over losing or releasing, which I think are all contributing factors to trauma that exists in my family in my relationship to my dad. Growing up was definitely, in a lot of respects a very tumultuous. As loving and generous as my father was, there was also this side of him that was kind of a bully. He had a lot of rage and anger that was unresolved and so he projected that... on everyone. He was definitely a power lover, so he needed to have that sense of power and control all the time.

That was a real part of our family dynamics. And, my mom was extremely passive and a full-on people pleaser. There was this dynamic that I saw, particularly between my father and mom. That power looked like my mom had very little agency, and particularly because my paternal grandparents controlled so much of who we are as a family - what we could do and how we functioned in the world. So, with that dynamic, and how my father could be punitive AKA The Punisher and call the shots... at a really early age I took on the role of protector - protecting my mom, my brother and myself. The truth of the matter is we are probably more alike than not. Also, very strong-willed in that kind of loud way.

My relationship with my father could be extremely combative. Particularly into my later adolescent teen years, we just fought and argued all the time. It was constant. And, I think over the years, the impact of who my father was on my sense of self, my sense of belonging, my sense of being enough, my sense of being lovable and worthy just decreased over time. So did my rage and anger towards my father.

My father grew up in an extreme sort of wealth and affluence and privilege and, without getting into all the family history and trauma, basically he grew up with servants and nannies. Extreme wealth but, ended up with not a pot to piss in and even a momentary blip of being homeless and nothing but his children at his side. When he died, which was sad and painful in a lot of ways BUT my father was sort of this slow deterioration of a human being. Full of constant broken promises and unhealed trauma only addressed with addictions. It was just so pathological. He never followed through; just broken promise after broken promise. And, my stepmom, (though they never legally married I called her my stepmom) Patty, died of cancer. When she died, that was when we really saw his situation for what it really was and who he really was. Before that, so many things were easily masked and it was easy to close our eyes. Once my father's money ran out my stepmom basically became the provider. She covered so many things and she took care of everything so there was less of a role to play. When she passed there was a lot of pain. There are roles that I had to step into like being the parent while he was the child. My step mom, as she was dying of cancer, begged me to help get him out of the house because she couldn't take it anymore.

When it came down to it, my parents liked chaos. When the shit hit the fan, they would act like they were functioning with an alter ego, especially my mom. She thrived on that. In the end, my dad showed up very beautifully for my step mom but, when she passed, he had nothing. He couldn't afford to live in their house anymore. We had to pack him up and move him out. A really tough part was his stubbornness and inability to humble himself. It was one thing after the other. My stepbrother owned a halfway house. He was a recovering drug addict and was very successful business wise. When he got clean, he said that my father could live there. Before he moved there he was renting a room from a man that eventually we had to deal with, like, almost going to the courts and all this stuff because he refused to leave and the guy plus my brother were desperately trying to get my dad out. He wasn't paying he was just a mess and again, almost on the streets. Then my stepbrother stepped in as his parent and had to speak to him like a child and get him to finally say yes to make the move. I did a lot of the emotional caretaking for my parents. I would say my older brother did the business side like what bills need to get paid, the laundry list of to dos, and handle my parents inability to function at times. There was a period where my older brother - which we knew was a significantly bad idea - moved in with him. I think that was the first place he went to maybe his second place. But that just turned out to be a fallen shit show. I mean just, horrific. So, all this stuff with my father as he diminished - the emotional pain. The feeling of abandonment and neglect of not having a father that could show up just got worse and worse and worse and worse, and the anger just grew and grew and grew. All of those dynamics that could be present. Then, my stepbrother actually ended up overdosing and dying. That meant a halfway house. He didn't actually do the healing he needed to do when my step mom passed. He got injured and took painkillers and then one thing led to another. So my dad basically squatted for like a year in this sort of abandoned halfway house while the estate was being handled. He got to live there rent free and then got booted out. That's when he had some health stuff. Something happened and we were concerned about the early stages of dementia. I don't remember all the details or the timeline but basically he ended up in a hospital. Nothing left, no home, no nothing. My older brother and I are done. We're not doing it. That's when my younger brother stepped in for the first time, who was not done, and wanted his daddy to live. We are blessed that he was able to stay in the hospital long enough. While they monitored him, my brother was able to get him into an assisted living facility, a state facility that social security covered, I guess. And that's where he finished off his life. I remember getting the call from the hospital. It was basically me having a conversation with the nurse and her being very frank that if we want to see our father, we should get on a plane. We met my brother in Florida who was transferring him to hospice. I remember just seeing him there. It's something to witness someone as they're getting ready to, you know... It's just really intense, but he seems so helpless and probably felt powerless. Just sitting there with him and crying because I'm angry because I'm sad because I don't even know why I'm crying. It was a couple of really divine universe things happening, as he transitioned the following morning. We are with him through the night, holding his hand by his side. We thought that stubborn man was going to actually go longer than he did. He ended up passing that next morning. Gratefully I was able to be by his side and see him take his last breath. I would say that the healing side of all this is when he took his last breath and I realized he had passed, transitioned. My brothers are talking to the doctor and I'm like, you know he's gone. I had this whole embodiment of like protecting him and holding him and my face was on his chest and wailing crying. My brother stood there with the doctor. I left the room. Then I had this really intense sensation, I don't even know what you would call it but something shooting through my body and out. And all of a sudden it was like this pure soul. That was laying there, that all these years of anger and pain and resentment and sadness, just lifted, just sort of came through my body and out like this existential experience. And I sat there like kind of knowing what was going on and also not going, knowing what was going on, but really feeling, you know him as this Divine Child of God, you know, just this, this pure being like the body was just sort of this vessel this shell but the soul what I believe is an eternal soul. I believe that a lot of what I experienced is because of years and years of every modality of healing work that I did. But there was also something for me in that moment that I don't even know if I could fully explain. It was like magic, even though it wasn't but that all sudden poof. I didn't feel my body. I felt lighter. I felt freer. It was like something just completely physically, mentally, emotionally, spiritually, opened up since then I haven't really felt any major, trauma from him or anger and pain. I'm connected to a lot of inner child work that I still need to be doing to address all my fears and projections and worries but I think it's now less to do about him and just recognizing that there's been some deep internalization of things that have gone on and that it's not so much the person, it's what I've internalized and really shifting that. So I'm grateful I can hold my father today with a tremendous amount of love and gratitude and not think he's the devil, or a God awful human being or an asshole. You don't have to have a lifetime of resentments. I now experience more gratitude and love and appreciation for who he was and all that he brought to our lives, and that I'm really grateful for.

The father/daughter dynamic is important and very delicate. For many reasons, daughters choose their future partners based on their fathers regardless of whether dad is present or absent. If there is a wound, and that wound is not healed, you run the risk of repeating the dysfunctional couplings of your parents and grandparents. We cannot heal what we do not confront. If damage has been done, healing this bond is necessary and can look very differently depending on your circumstances. If you have access to your father, consider having conversations to discuss your experiences. Maybe even construct a timeline of events that made an impact and process together. Caveat: If your father is dangerous, has a history of abusing you and/or has a personality disorder, I'd advise against meeting. Emotionally dangerous and unavailable people will never appreciate your pain, needs and grievances. Your emotional experience will likely will fall on deaf ears because sociopaths don't admit their mistakes because they aren't mature enough to see the advantage of being honest, transparent and vulnerable.

If contact isn't safe, or if your father is deceased, you can write a letter to him to process your experiences and validate them for yourself. Make sure to include all the significant events that you remember. If you decide to share your letter (you don't have to), it's important to set boundaries with him before you meet.

These boundaries are important for yourself more than him. You need to protect yourself in these situations. If he doesn't agree to your rules, no meeting. Remember, you don't have to do this. This is a very risky situation so keep your expectations in check. You may not get the apology you are looking for. You most likely won't. This reunification act should be initiated by the perpetrator not the victim but, usually that never happens. Again, it isn't the child's responsibility to initiate the repair. If you feel you're doing too much work you probably are.

No one outside of you will ever know how it feels to be you. Even if your father is willing to try, he will never understand the pain or confusion he caused, so don't set yourself up for disappointment when he doesn't deliver the reaction and response you want. It takes an emotionally mature person to be willing to engage in conversations like this. If your dad isn't emotionally mature, mind your expectations. In some instances, you should prepare for your request to be denied. Regardless of his engagement in conversations you can still heal yourself by yourself. When listing all the significant events, include how you felt in the moment. Express who comforted you and, if they didn't, how you wish they had. Allow yourself time to embrace all that you have experienced and endured. Forgive your father for not valuing you because he probably doesn't value himself. Forgive yourself for perpetuating any of the same behaviors with your own kids and change yourself in order to validate their experiences. Grieve what should have been. Celebrate the healthy future that awaits your descendants through your choice of healthy parenting of your own children.

Alex's Story

When my parents separated, then divorced it was just before I started middle school. My mother eventually moved away leaving us with our dad. They asked me if it was okay that she moved.

~ 51 ~

Only now do I realize what a shitty position they put me in. Asking for my permission to leave was so inappropriate. Looking back, I realize as a family we never recovered. How could I say no? I could tell she wanted to leave so I said it was okay. That set me up to be people-pleaser for decades.

I didn't realize at the time but my dad had already mentally checked out. That had to be a big reason why she wanted to leave. He wasn't a partner, he wasn't a father, he was an alcoholic. I like to think he tried his best to raise me and my siblings but how well could he actually do in that state of mind? Whenever my mother would call there was this combination of desperately missing her and being so pissed off at the same exact time. What parent voluntarily leaves their children? It was easy to be mad at her because her presence was gone. Only as an adult did I realize my father had left us first by choosing alcohol. He was physically there but emotionally abandoned us after he'd abandoned himself. I think he thought he didn't have to do more than pay bills because at least he was there. Kids need more than that. He never shared anything about himself, his own childhood was a mystery to us. I can only guess he had less than we did which is why he gave us so little. He was always drunk. My older brother raised us. I see him as my parent more than my mother or father. I celebrate him on Father's Day. I really hate Father's Day and Mother's Day.

I don't know what intimacy feels like other than being afraid of it. It's scary so I'd rather date a bunch of women than have one that knows everything about me. I don't know how to have a relationship. It took a long time to realize I give out the same crumbs I was given.

Charlotte's Father

I remember riding on my dad's lap steering his Jeep while he worked the gas and brake pedals. Mostly, we would ride together in the daytime, but I fondly remember him letting me drive at night. I was never afraid and always on the lookout for whatever animals could potentially jump in front of the car and scare me as I was "driving."

Life with my dad is a good time. I love him and appreciate everything that he has passed onto me. I have learned how to check the oil and tires on my cars, select a decent six pack of beer, and to always laugh. I grew up with this whimsical view of my dad as someone who could make mistakes, but he would never and could never hurt me. It's disheartening, as his daughter, to know that he and my mother have been abandoned or neglected by their parents. I appreciate them both because I never have felt these feelings or had the same experiences.

I remember when my parents separated then divorced and he made sure to visit me on weekends and holidays. I wish I could ignore the hours and sometimes days that would pass by before he would be there to pick me up. The excitement that built up inside me would soon burst as soon as I saw him pulling into the driveway in his latest truck. The tickle of his mustache when he kisses my face all over still brings me an immense amount of joy. I do not think anyone loves him as much as I do. I know this because I am his shield. Even if he does not know it. I protect him and honor him because he is mine and I am his.

My perspective of my father has always been the same. A provider, protector, and a man who is human. My father is someone's child, just as I am his child. I understood this growing up because I was close to his mother, but not in the ways he has experienced closeness with her, or lack thereof. I recognize that my father has unhealed wounds from generational trauma. I understand I cannot view my father through only the lens of his daughter. Now I am a woman, still a daughter but not a child. My father loves me in the capacity he knows how, and I love him back in my own capacity.

My father and I have always had different opinions politically and socially. But in the last few years he's taken it to a new level. I don't go home anymore. He has been waving the QAnon flag for a while now. It's utterly embarrassing. How I came from him, I have no idea. My close friends know about him but I don't tell anyone else. For some reason the insurrection shook him out of his stupidity and now he's trying to make amends. I don't know how I can forgive him.

Every single parent hopes they're making the right decisions. And we all make decisions based on all the information we have at that moment. It's important for each side to explain the motivations behind their decisions. Those explanations usually reveal fear of some kind. Opening the door to these vulnerable conversations will introduce compassion to the dialogue. If you decide to do things differently than how you were taught, be prepared for the emotions that surface, typically guilt and fear of appearing disrespectful or being ostracized by your family.

Challenging your family's method of doing things is difficult but necessary. We love them but can be hesitant to go against their teachings. In the words of Maya Angelou, "When you know better, do better." It takes courage and determination to do things differently than you were taught.

Working with Clients

Tarah

Tarah and her younger brother were born to drug addicts with untreated mental illness. The root of most adult substance use is childhood abuse at the hands of an addicted parent. It should be noted that 85% of all drug addicts experienced some type of abuse in their childhoods and, children who are abused are typically raised by parents with no distress tolerance and maladaptive coping mechanisms. That cycle continues with each generation raised under these circumstances. Per the National Clearinghouse of Alcohol and Drug Information, children of alcoholics are 2-4 times more likely than non children of alcoholics to develop alcoholism.

At an early age, Tarah's grandmother stepped in to raise her and her brother due to their parents spiraling into chemical dependency. As Tarah grew up, she felt more comfortable confronting her parents' destructive behavior. I started working with her at 15 years old and have continued working with her off and on into her 20's. During that time her mother got clean, met a new partner (a newly recovering addict) and had another baby, Tarah's 4th sibling.

During this time, another of Tarah's half-siblings, was discovered to have been molested by his half-brother who was also being raised by a grandmother. Upon discovery, Tarah rescued her little brother and started raising him, without support from either of his parents. Tarah was only 20 years old. Tarah's father did not offer any financial support or time where she could take a break from raising HIS child. After 9 months, and her own mental health failing, Tarah had to take a stand. She, with the support of her grandmother, forced her father to take care of his son. Tarah knew this would damage the often tenuous relationship with her father but she realized her stability had never been his priority.

During one of our last sessions, Tarah shared, "I haven't talked to my dad in a while. I really don't care if I ever talk to him again. He got his latest girlfriend pregnant again, moved in with her, then moved out." There are so many layers to the dysfunction drug addiction perpetuates and the ripple effect of neglect, crime, abandonment and untreated mental illness can lay a path of destruction for years to come. Despite substance abuse wrecking multiple generations of her family, Tarah remained resolute in breaking the grip of mental illness, chemical dependency and underachievement in her family. She recently enrolled in a 4-year college. She'll be the first in her family to graduate. She has no relationship with her father at this time.

Lindsey

Lindsey was referred to me by a former client. I helped that client process childhood trauma and build boundaries with her family. Then she thought I could help her friend Lindsey do the same. Since we began, Lindsey has referred other clients to me as well. Lindsey reminds me of so many of my adult clients. She's a resilient and productive perfectionist who experienced "strange" moments where she felt she was "too" emotional without provocation. As a perfectionist she didn't know why her small children and husband would not cooperate. She loved them but didn't see them. Her childhood was marred with sexual and emotional neglect which resulted in being shamed and disconnected by her parents. She was not nurtured, had no guidance because her father put all of his attention and energy into his church. Subconsciously, Lindsey decided her family had to be perfect to make up for her lack of perfection growing up.

Lindsey's parents divorced when she was very young. She and her siblings were raised by their father, a minister. Her brother had medical issues throughout his childhood. As he got progressively sicker, their father said her brother's illness was because he broke a house rule and/or didn't obey God. He was rigid, self-righteous and clueless about protecting his kids. Lindsey had no female guidance and through her father's rantings was taught that if anything goes wrong it's the girl/woman's fault. At 13 years old, Lindsey was lured to a home by an older teenager and sexually assaulted. When she told her father about being held down by the teenager, an older boy she thought would be her boyfriend, and raped, her father told her that was her fault too.

Like most people raised in the church, Lindsey was raised to swallow the gospel whole without question. Doing that meant she carried the most horrible level of shame for "having sex out of wedlock". Our work consisted of assigning shame to the rightful party, the adults who preyed on children, the adults who don't protect children. Their relationship was practically non-existent. In Lindsey's late teens and early 20s she had a series of toxic relationships with men that left her feeling worthless. She eventually confronted her father by asking him for a timeline of all the major events of her childhood. Surprisingly he complied but did not consider she may have created her own timeline. Guess what? Their timelines didn't match up. As they discussed the discrepancies her father dismissed or diminished several major events that shaped Lindsey's identity and how she saw herself in the world. She knew they'd never get on the same page because people usually never know how much they're hurting others. She healed by reading, processing and writing about everything she'd gone through. She had always thought she was the weakling in her relationship. Then she realized her father would never allow himself to admit how he had failed her. She was stronger than him and was the head of a healthy, positive and loving family.

Although I'm not a parent I'm the child of parents who didn't do their jobs well. My father and mother divorced when I was three. He went on to remarry twice; each time forgetting the former family in favor of the current. My youngest step-brother and I have completely different views of the same man. A while back I'd made a social media post about a recent career accomplishment. My step-brother made a comment about how proud our father would be. In a brief offline conversation, I made clear that we experienced very different versions of our father. All that I've accomplished is in spite of him, not because of him. (Yeah, I've still got some healing to do.)

There are no perfect parents and no perfect childhoods. I've found that the perfectionists of the world have chronic anxiety born in childhood trauma whether they want to admit it or not. Perfectionism has many different root causes but one is grow-ing up in an environment of emotional neglect and uncertainty. Kids that grow up with chaotic or neglectful parents, can de-velop a negative self-image, have low self-esteem which can lead to an unquenched desire to prove their worth. 'If I make straight As, she will love me.' 'If I'm the best football player dad won't hurt me.' If this sounds familiar to you your healing jour-ney should include re-parenting yourself and addressing your inner child and relational trauma wounds. The therapeutic re-lationship aids in this process. Therapists can function as sub-stitute parents during sessions.

Therapists function as sounding boards to process and heal. I believe most of what we do includes helping people realize they aren't the only ones experiencing anything and every-thing. The situation that keeps you up at night, causes crying and worry, is indeed disappointing, shocking and/or frustrat-ing.

Betsy

Aside from being an only child, Betsy's story is very close to my own. Betsy was born to a narcissistic mother and ineffectual father. Her childhood was either spent alone or with parents who acted like they had something better to do than raise her. Loving each other was a memory. One night, at 3 years old, she awoke to find the house was empty. She wandered around her apartment then the interior of her building. She said she went back to the apartment but didn't cry until she sat for several minutes then realized her parents weren't close or coming back soon. This moment and, unfortunately, many others taught Betsy that she could not expect her parents to protect her and she couldn't count on them to understand her needs. "My parents are supposed to love and protect me. I needed protection from them." Internalizing this moment of abandonment, fear, not being valued or protected sent her on a decades-long anxiety and a desperate desire to control everything in her surroundings. She questioned everything and everyone, doubted herself and feared doing even the slightest things that could cause someone to leave her or leave herself unstable like being fired.

Betsy and I walked through her childhood together to dismantle the limiting beliefs she had which affected her relationships and career. Upon reflection it turns out her father was constantly abandoning her. His perspective was 'I had it hard so everyone else should too.' Sounds pretty harsh especially considering he left his daughter when she was 10 years old with her mother/ his wife he felt "ruined" his life. If he felt her unbearable, how could a child survive that?

Each parent engaged in gaslighting her before that was even a mainstream concept. She questioned everything and everyone but, mostly herself. She didn't trust anyone including herself. At times her anxiety was debilitating especially when dealing with her father. She learned to lean into the facts of a situation instead of spiraling while preparing for the worst-case scenario. She learned to create boundaries for her father that he always said he would respect but never did. His repeated disrespect forced her to acknowledge that her father didn't value her the way she deserved. By validating and normalizing her childhood trauma, she learned coping skills and her self-worth increased. She stopped ruminating over every single interaction and she eventually gained the courage to stand up for herself and sever ties with her father. The strength she felt from handling that situation flowed to her job as well. She felt less desire to do everything perfectly and didn't ruminate on every work conversation in her head in order to self-criticize.

Sometimes she felt guilty thinking, "Should I really cut him off? He's old and could die soon." That would eventually fade after she started creating boundaries with herself. She stopped putting others' needs ahead of her own. She had to grieve in order to level out the anger and disappointment. She looked at the good things her father gave her: height, eye color, athleticism, whatever. She decided to focus on the positives rather than marinate in anger and frustration. He didn't father her when she was most vulnerable in childhood. Why assume he'd be a better man in her adulthood.

At this point Betsy has severed ties with her father. He still calls and leaves voicemails delivering cheap shots at her about the things that are important to her: politics, mental health, climate change, etc. She is getting more comfortable deleting the voicemails before listening to them. It's a process and she's giving herself grace. She was groomed to blindly honor her father so it's been difficult releasing that programming. But she's giving herself the space to think in a new way. She realizes her duty to him can stop because he never honored his duty her.

CHAPTER 4

Mothers

The expectations placed on mothers are unrealistic and can also be disrespectful and dismissive. Yet, becoming a mother seems to be a foregone conclusion for many women, whether they want it or not. I think having children is the most demanding job in the world. You are constantly serving, protecting, and teaching in a society that seems hellbent on destroying any semblance of peace, innocence, and structure. On any given day, you can watch the news and see child abuse reports of mothers and fathers whom I can only assume thought they were rocking the parenting game. So many people are ill-equipped mentally, spiritually, and or financially yet crank out multiple children when that is the last thing they should be doing. The pressure placed on women to procreate needs to stop. The shame delivered to women who decide not to have babies needs to stop. Nearly every adult client I have is in therapy because of the damage done by their mothers and fathers in childhood. As a society, we must stop assuming motherhood (and marriage) are necessary rites of passage that give a woman value.

Unfortunately, generations of women are forced into this role due to a lack of birth control, needing the resources of a male partner for survival, or both. The children they birth cannot articulate feeling unwanted, not being a priority, and feeling like a burden. The low self-worth and low self-esteem this causes can last a lifetime and will impact every part of the child's life into adulthood. Although some mothers can disguise their resentment, some cannot, and the child feels it. Some mothers create reasons to justify why they've hurt their children. Some mothers abuse their children and then create reasons to hate their children when reminded of the pain they've caused their children. The child becomes the scapegoat. This is a tactic utilized by some mothers to justify their cruelty and assuage their guilt.

Being raised by a mother who doesn't want you, dismisses you, and neglects your needs is devastating. I know - This was my childhood. The assumptions are overwhelming. It is an ignorant assumption that all women want to be mothers. It is also an assumption that once a woman assumes the role, they love it. Talk about peer pressure! Several years ago, a guest on the Oprah Winfrey talk show, who was married with 3 or 4 children, told the audience that she loved her husband more than her children. The women in the audience crucified her. Her stance was that her relationship with her husband started first, and becoming a mom could not have happened without him, her primary relationship. She also said the security and happiness in the home couldn't happen without him, and she appreciated that. The audience became unglued. How dare she love her husband before her children. I think they drank the Kool-Aid flavored 'Motherhood is the best thing that will ever happen to me!' or 'My children are my world!' and, 'I don't want to do anything but serve my children.' Motherhood is a very personal decision and a nuanced role. Please stay in your own backyard and stop shaming women who choose to do life differently.

I was on a trip overseas and had an enlightening conversation with our tour guide over lunch. As a therapist, our discussion deepened quickly because that's how I roll. I asked him about women's place in the workforce in his country because it seemed like men had nearly all of the jobs, even outside of positions of power. I noticed that the few women with jobs were usually young, in their teens or early 20s. The guide said that if a woman was not married early, she worked until she found a husband. Once married, the woman quit because her new job was to have children and care for the home. I asked what happened to the women who chose not to marry or bear children. He said those kinds of women didn't exist. I was disappointed but not shocked by his response, being a college-educated woman who is also a business owner, who received several marriage proposals but waited to marry until 40 years old. I asked how he knew they didn't exist. He was confident that women only wanted marriage and children. I challenged him by asking, "How do you know that's all women want when you've taken away their other options?" He was silent. I assume his silence was due to being openly challenged by a single black, self-sufficient woman in her 40s, proudly having sex whenever she wanted with no desire to have children. Our conversation hit a brick wall after I told him not every woman wants to be a mother, nor should every woman be a mother.

Becoming pregnant does not magically instill healthy mothering skills in a woman. Some women never acquire the ability to love, nurture, protect, or guide a child. When your job isn't what you expected, no one bats an eye if you decide to quit. Motherhood is hyped as the ultimate dream job, and women do not have any other acceptable ways to describe it except blissful and the 'best job on the planet'. It is a job but one you can never quit. You can't even ask for help without fearing judgment. If you're unhappy with the role or its circumstances, there's seemingly no escape. You have to grin and bear it all while the child suffers the consequences. We need to normalize not having children.

Being raised by a mother who should not be one is torture figuratively and, unfortunately, literally in some cases. You know when you're unwanted, you can understand when you're not a priority, and can feel when you're being abused no matter how young you are. Your heart and mind record it. You feel all of it, and those wounds can last a lifetime. Those wounds will affect how you experience love, how you feel about yourself, and how you parent if you decide to have children. I beg anyone who chooses to parent to go through therapy FIRST. Heal as much as you can because you will get triggered in ways you can't imagine as soon as you become a parent. Heal your attachment issues, heal your emotional and abandonment trauma, heal your physical and sexual trauma. You will pass on unhealthy patterns to future generations if you don't. What we don't heal, we are destined to repeat.

A Letter to Walter's Mother

Mom, I've avoided this long enough...

I have your voice etched into my brain with your too-often-spoken phrase & it's been ripping me apart for as long as I can remember. No matter how much I try to reason past it, I know it's not true intellectually. But still, I can never let it go. Anytime anything goes wrong in my life or that of someone I love, I hear your voice & blame myself... It's fucking ludicrous, it's fucking obscene, but I still blame myself as though I can affect such things. Nevertheless, I fall right back into that doubt and that immense guilt.

"You cried so much and brought this upon us, and now your father is dead!

Your brothers are abroad! Which one of them do you want to die next?!"

You said that to me so often; it feels like you must have said it every day of my life from the time you got home from the hospital to my early teens... "You cried so much and brought this upon us & now your father is dead! Your brothers are abroad; which one of them do you want to die next?!" It rings in my head like you are in the same room with me now.

I wish I could give it the proper gravity that your choice of words gives this phrase in Arabic. English doesn't do it any justice. It still hits me like a gigantic hammer in the chest. If planting this guilt bomb into my brain from the time I was five years old, like the soundtrack of my childhood, wasn't enough, you always had to put me down.

I was never good enough at anything. If I got great grades, there would always be a complaint and a reminder that I'm ordinary and not smarter than anyone else. If anyone paid me a compliment about how I looked, you would remind me that I was no more special than anyone else and not to buy into people's politeness or let it go to my head.

It's not that I'm not grateful for how you took care of me. I know you're a product of your childhood. I can't say that I know what happened to you, but from what little I know, I'm sure it sucked! You wouldn't share anything of worth from your childhood... You wouldn't even tell me when your birthday was because you didn't deserve to celebrate after your husband died, obviously because I killed him. Don't worry... I'll never forget! You made sure of that!!! I know that if it weren't for you and how much you did with what little we had in the middle of a civil war, I wouldn't be here today. I should've died well over a dozen times with all of the shit we went through. How many literal bullets I've dodged is mind-boggling to say the least. You are overprotective and wouldn't let me do anything or have friends. To this day, I always question when someone wants to be my friend... I always doubt their sincerity. Why would they want to be my friend? They must want something from me. Or is it because I do things for them???

I hate how things ended between us, and how much I wish you didn't have such a dark cloud constantly hanging over you. I wish you didn't push everyone away. I wish you would allow yourself to smile or laugh. I hardly have any memories of you laughing or smiling. You are always this sad woman wearing black & making sure that I was in that darkness with you. I wish you let our lives be about something other than your tragedy. You lost your husband because of some fucking asshole that decided to get drunk off his ass and go for a drive. IT FUCKING SUCKS, I know! Your whole entire world came apart at the seams. Your entire identity was shattered in an instant... I get it. If something happened to my wife, I would be even more broken and lost... I wouldn't survive it, of that I'm sure... but I don't have a five-year-old to be there for... You did! As much as you liked to portray yourself as this holier than though, selfless and giving martyr, you were very fucking selfish! You made everything about you! Life fucked you, and you kept punishing everyone in your circle for it. As the youngest, I was the closest to your fire, and you made sure that I was on fire, too. I couldn't just be a fucking kid. You are a wronged widow, and it was all about how much of a victim YOU are.

The fucked up thing is, I've already forgiven you, but, I can't let go of my programming as irrational as it is! I like to think of myself as a very rational person, so this really fucks with my brain. I don't believe in anything supernatural, but for some fucking reason, I still blame myself for shit that happens to those around me... 'Sandy gets a brain tumor; I wonder what I did to bring it on'. WHAT?!!! I'm thinking, "What did I do to cause my sister to get a brain tumor?!" I know that I'm being irrational, and this really fucks with my brain. Your programming has been very difficult to rewrite, but I'm finally getting help because I can't get rid of it on my own, and I have fucking tried.

While I'm on a roll, there's a conversation or an attempted one that sticks out in my mind. I've replayed it a few times over the years. I'm sure my memory of it is flawed, but it was after Mike confronted you with what you used to say to me on a regular basis. After he quoted it to you, in your tone no less, you told him that you had no memory of ever saying that to me! I'm not going to lie, but that shit hurt me almost as much as your catchphrase. 'You cried so much and brought this upon us, and now your father is dead! Your brothers are abroad; which one of them do you want to die next?!' You engraved this fucking scar into my brain, and you don't even fucking remember it?!!! Are you fucking kidding me?! Seriously, you said this to me hundreds of times, but you can't be bothered to remember it?! That was one of the last times you and Mitch talked because you had to chase him out of your life. Was it because he called you out on all of your bullshit? He was the only one of us that stood up to you. You couldn't stand that! You had to cut him out of your life, and you tried to guilt me with it. You tried to make me choose between you two. How fucked up is that?! I'm so glad I stood up to you and told you that you would never talk to me about him again if you wanted me in your life. I think I scared you when I did that. I think it really surprised you that I stood up to you and said no.

I remember the rage that started building inside me when you opened up that topic in your attempt at an apology. You said that you couldn't remember saying it, and then you actually started to say it. You are actually about to say your catchphrase. I don't know what I would have done had I let you. I don't know if I would have broken down like I was five years old or if I would have hurt you. I honestly don't know. I have no idea. Part of me is frightened of what I may have done. I felt so much pain and rage, but I managed to tell you to stop and not to say another. I was actually calm and didn't yell. I just said stop. I would like to think that the tears that you had in your eyes are real and that you are truly sorry for your past actions, but I don't know that. You are such a master manipulator! You could teach a class on the topic, just brilliant! Maybe the tears are real, maybe you didn't remember, and your words are just a passing thing from your perspective that you just said without thought.

One decision that I'm so happy that I made was not exposing my wife, Lauren, to you. That makes me so sad to say. I hate that not introducing the most important person in my life to you was the right thing to do. How fucked up is that? But you earned that. I introduced you to one girl that I dated and in doing so, confirmed that I was right not to have introduced you to any other one. You chased her away so fast and caused me so much pain at the time. She was being kind to you and tried to befriend you, but you couldn't help yourself.

You had to lecture her and teach her how to treat me. No wonder she ran for the hills. Who could blame her? As it turns out, though, it led me to Lauren and the lesson to keep her away from you. Since I am on this topic... When the fuck did you become racist? I knew enough that introducing you to her while we were just dating would be a bad idea. After all, nobody was ever good enough for any of your sons, which is so fucking bizarre to me because you always went out of your way to tell all of us that we were nothing special and 'just like everybody else.' So, why was there never a girl or woman good enough for any of us? After asking Lauren to marry me, you are the last person I told. Somehow, I knew that you would find a way to burst my bubble, but I had no idea that you would go where you did.

My original idea was to tell you that I was coming to visit and bring her with me. I'm so glad I thought better of it. After getting advice from Doug, I called you on my way home. I was feeling joyful and wanted to share the news with you that I was going to get married. I expected some guilting, of course. You could always find a way to guilt me, and that's exactly what you did. Instead, this time you went in a different direction. From all of my memories, I can't recall you ever saying anything bad about black people. Not a single thing. In fact, I remember you talking fondly of the Liberians that you know and employed in Liberia. You would go to great lengths to show how amazing their work ethic was and how well they would make your recipes. You praised them every time the topic came up. I never expected you to lose your shit over the fact that I had dated, proposed to & was about to marry a black woman. I remember that drive so well, your rejection of her before you had laid your eyes on her or had a single conversation with her. I asked you if her being black makes her any less of a person, you actually said yes... I'm still shocked! I remember it like an out-of-body experience! When I told you not to make me choose between the two of you, I remember my words exactly... "Are you saying that if I'm with her, you won't be in my life?" You shocked me again by saying, yes.

So, I guess you're out of my life. I said goodbye, and I hung up the phone. I don't know if you cried after I hung up, but I did. I pulled over and sobbed like a little boy again. I wonder who I killed or what tragedy I brought upon the world by doing that? I'm not going to get into how embarrassing it was for me not to have my mother at my wedding. Having to explain it to my new family that embraced me with so much warmth, love, and affection. Lauren's mother has shown me so much love, and it makes me sad for you. You could've been part of so much love.

Like I said, I think I've already forgiven you. I wish you could be forgiving, but you don't have it in you. I wish you had a better childhood. Perhaps you need to be medicated, and that could make a difference. I wish you didn't have so much tragedy in your life. From losing so many of your siblings, losing your first child when she was a baby, losing your husband with a five-year-old child to raise on your own, to losing another child to a brain tumor when she was only thirty. Yes, it's unfair and tragic. It Fucking Sucks! I also wish you found a different way to cope with your tragedies. I wish I weren't your emotional punching bag or physical one, either. There aren't many beatings, but they are memorable! I wish that you could have been part of our lives in a more positive way. It's time for me to let this shit go... I don't know how to... but it's time...

Thank you for all that you did to help us survive; you were amazing at it, you truly were. I still don't know how you made what little money we had stretch so much. It's time for me to do more than just survive though.

Kelly's Mother

My mom has been in a memory care home for a while. But, because of Covid, I had to get her out. I brought her to live with me, which I was really excited about but, it's been so weird. She isn't who I remember. She isn't the jet setting actress entertaining people around the world. She isn't the attentive and tireless mother who could run circles around all the other moms. She's tired. She's nervous. She's forgetful.

My sister lives in a different country and doesn't understand how hard it is to take care of her by myself. And, on top of the lack of understanding, she's bitchy about every decision I make regardless of not being here to help at all. So, as I take care of our mother, I'm also taking care of my sister's immaturity from a different hemisphere. And I don't know what to do. I don't know if what I'm doing is right. I would go to her when I didn't know what to do with my life. Who do I go to now when I don't know what to do with hers?

She has dementia. The cognitive decline has been intense. I don't know what type of therapy to get her. Music, art, or drama therapy? CBT? CPT? DBT - They all sound the same! Don't get me started on the medications. This is hard. What would she do?

My dad died years ago, so my mom had a fiancé,' until recently. They got engaged, then he passed away. She's chewing her fingers to the quick. I think she's anxious, but I can only imagine why. I'm not even sure she's aware of what she's doing.

I'm not built for this caregiver stuff. It's hard to see a woman who was so powerful need help going to the bathroom. She's declining every day and I just want someone else to handle it. She's so sweet, but I get frustrated. I'm such an asshole. I need to be patient with her. I guess I need to be patient with myself, too.

Alzheimer's is a horrific disease. As the disease progress, the person you knew slowly disappears. A part of that process can include forgetfulness, irritability, physical deterioration, and violence. Regardless of the disease presentation, you are allowed to create new boundaries for a parent who no longer presents in a healthy, coherent way.

Many in the mental health community feel suppressed and unhealed childhood trauma can surface in the violence seen in aging people suffering from Alzheimer's and dementia. Yelling, screaming, physical aggression, Sundowner's – all could be connected to childhood abuse that the person was able to hide or suppress but can no longer due to cognitive decline.

Michelle and Her Mother

Driving into the Sonoran Desert after fleeing the disaster that is Las Vegas, the saguaro cactus warmly welcomed me with their waving arms - the friendliest experience I'd had in days. The aforementioned disaster in Vegas was not losing excessive amounts of money at the casinos, or partying into oblivion. Nope, the disaster was my mother.

In my family of five, I am considered "the rock," or at least that is what one of my therapists determined after months of dissection. The family turns to me to be the peacemaker, the responsible one, the one who demonstrates acceptable behavior. I'm not exceptional in any way, it's simply based on comparison in this tiny subset of the human population. So, when I arrived on my mother's doorstep in Las Vegas, heartbroken, crying, and devastated from breaking up with my fiance', my Mom didn't know how to handle this crushed version of me.

My expectation was that I would be consumed by empathetic, deeply caring, compassionate arms holding me tightly to her in the shared knowing of loss. Instead, 'antagonistic' does not describe the next ten days that I stayed with her until I escaped to Arizona under the false story that I had to attend a work conference.

During those ten days, Mom consumed more than one handle of Jose Cuervo, pounded on my bedroom door during conference calls that I was leading, and required that I deep clean the condo, including the bathrooms, before leaving. In order to work, my parents connected WiFi, of which I was required to foot the bill. This would seem reasonable under normal circumstances, except that a double standard was now in play. My parents often covered my sister's veterinary bills, dining out, mortgage payments, landscaping, and many other expenses I was unaware of. Yet I was required to pay back the extra $30 for WiFi.

Oh, and the fights. Emotionally, I was destroyed by breaking off my engagement with a man I deeply loved. When I was met with hostility, I lost it. In my lifetime, I don't think I screamed as loudly or forcefully as I did at my Mom during that time or at my dad while he was on the phone defending my mother's behavior. I was belligerent. I felt so much anger towards them, the circumstances, and the world that I felt inky black inside. I could not understand why they weren't helping me through this crisis. I was effectively homeless after leaving my fiance. The safe shelter I thought I was arriving to ended up being an inhospitable, volatile, unwelcoming warzone. So, I left and didn't speak with my family for an entire year.

Working through the healing process during that year was a true turning point. As I mentioned, I was furious at my parents and my family for their lack of support during the lowest point of my life when I was always there for them. It felt like I was an inconvenience for having a problem. It felt like I wasn't allowed to need help, that I was purely the giver of help, and that I should never be the taker. Reciprocity, apparently, wasn't an option for me - I was required to be strong, independent, self-sufficient, and unwavering at all times. That expectation is genuinely exhausting.

I maintained strong negative feelings towards my family for most of that year. I wanted nothing to do with them. My Mom would call my aunt to ask about me via my cousin, who I was staying with. I felt I needed to build a barrier between me and my Mom to protect myself against additional rejection and pain. It was my coping mechanism. It felt good to remove myself from the responsibility of the role I historically played within my family unit my entire life.

Towards the end of that year, after much thought, inner reflection, and reading, I came to the conclusion that I no longer wanted to harbor such anger and resentment towards my Mom, dad, and siblings. Yes, they hurt me very deeply, and we had not discussed or resolved anything that had happened. But I realized that I was only hurting myself at that point. My black inky heart limited me, the emotional wall I constructed inhibited other relationships, and the constant low level of anger I harbored impacted my life experiences. I decided to choose forgiveness.

When I reflected on how I wanted to live my life, I imagined love, kindness, and exuberance. Barriers, walls, and rules cut me off from areas that are meant to be lived. It occurred to me that my expectations of my Mom and family played a critical role in the cause of my disappointment. I now know some of my mother's demons and it seems like I was set up for failure. Deciding to take ownership of my role in creating the venom in my soul was enormously powerful. Instead of blaming, I took responsibility for my part. Instead of waiting for an apology, I took ownership. Instead of being the victim, I became empowered.

I had to meet my Mom where she was and build a relationship on that common denominator of a foundation. What I expected and desired, she was not capable of. This isn't an insult. It's simply a fact based on our own lived experiences. I'm sure there are better analogies, but the one that makes sense to me was synonymous with being angry at someone who doesn't know a foreign language. If the person did not learn to speak another language, how can one be justifiably angry with that person? It's simply that the person does not understand or know how to practice it. It's not emotionally charged; it just is, even if it is unfortunate. Realizing that she had limitations changed my perspective on the situation, which changed everything for us. Until then, I believed my Mom was infallible in many ways.

As I began to reach out and rebuild our relationship, I began celebrating my Mom for all the goodness she possessed and the benefits she offered throughout my life. My gratitude for everything she did for me and all the sacrifices she made for me is overflowing. Shifting to an appreciation mindset for what she *does* bring and what she *does* offer, instead of resentment for what she doesn't, has created a space where we now have the closest relationship we've ever had.

Additionally, asking questions and learning more about the challenges she faced during her childhood made me realize she is one of the toughest, most resilient women I've ever known. She remains optimistic and buoyant despite many tragic and traumatic circumstances throughout her lifetime. Learning more about her, and how she dealt with animosity offered insight into why she may not be available in the way I wish during my devastating situations (luckily, there have been few).

We never revisited my time in Vegas, and it's okay. I do not see how rehashing that awful experience would benefit us because we would be at an impasse - me asking why she wasn't there for me and not receiving a satisfactory response. My therapists may disagree with this approach, but it works for us. Accepting the limits of our relationship allows me to know where the boundaries lie, which prevents me from establishing unattainable expectations that cause riffs between us. Loving her for who she is and building a strong relationship on what she is capable of brings me great joy and satisfaction. I love my Mom and am so grateful to have her as my mother. This experience offered a unique opportunity to learn the power of forgiveness and has significantly improved my life. For that, I am truly grateful.

Being the child of an alcoholic or addict presents unique challenges. When sober, one side of the parent's personality is present, when intoxicated you see someone else. Unfortunately, you have to arm yourself for all presentations. Many choose to end relationships with their parents due to the inconsistencies in reliability, presentation, harm done. If you decide to continue connecting make sure you don't enable their behavior. You can not love someone out of their addictions. No amount of money, time or housing will spare them from themselves. The hardest thing for a child of an addict to understand is your parent loves you to the level they are capable. Yes, they probably love you and they also love the substance. The substance allows them to numb themselves to their behavior, the harm that was done to them and how they have affected you. It's not as cut and dry to say your parent loves the substance more than you. It absolutely looks that way but shame is powerful. Many are so ashamed of their behavior they feel they will never be forgiven for it.

Working with Clients

Kate and Ashley

Teenage clients Kate and Ashley have mothers with untreated mental illness. Their mothers have never acknowledged how their behavior has affected how each girl was parented. Kate has lived with her father and stepmother since 5-years old when her mother had an incredibly explosive bipolar episode. According to the parenting plan, she had to visit her mother regularly on weekends until her late teenage years, when she could legally decline. Her mother's schizophrenia and bipolar were becoming more severe, and her mother's denial of increasing acuity. Kate made multiple unsuccessful attempts to set boundaries with her mother about college choices, visits, and communication to keep the peace. She knew her mother loved her but was also very ill. Kate learned when to negotiate (agreeing to apply to her mother's alma mater) and when to stand firm (not riding in the same car or communicating excessively while at school). Kate had to mourn the traditional events that would most likely not happen because it was not on the horizon for her mother to be a healthy participant in her life. The fear she felt before and during her high school graduation was something we had to work through. Her father stepped up beautifully. He enrolled her in therapy to manage her severe anxiety. He made changes within himself that made her comfortable discussing everything with him, including sex, piercings, having a girlfriend, etc.

Ashley was in a different situation. It was just her and her mother without the buffer of other healthy relatives. It was as if they were on an island by themselves. Ashley's mother was a narcissist with borderline personality disorder - a complex combination because she was constantly forced to manage and accept her mother's feelings while dismissing her own. She even became jealous and worried when Ashley and I had sessions. Ashley felt very isolated and trapped, so we leaned into coping skills to help her prepare for her independence and allow her to navigate sharing space with her mother. I had to straddle the line between validating her experiences without going too far into the misery of a situation that would not change for years until she could move out. I provided psychoeducation on her mother's diagnosis, which helped Ashley understand what could have caused her mother's behavior and why it was so difficult to change. This helped Ashley build compassion and understanding for her mother and have realistic expectations of her mother's capabilities so resentments wouldn't build when she fell short of Ashley's expectations. Ashley also looked within her community to find positive female role models who could give her the guidance and support she needed.

Nicole

Nicole became my client to process emotions connected to abuse experienced by a past parent. It was a domestic violence relationship; although she could walk away from it, she still felt the ripple effects of living in fear for so long. As we talked about her hypervigilance, fear of dating, and desire to go to college, we talked about her childhood.

Nicole was the oldest of three girls in the second set of children her mother raised alone. Nicole's childhood was spent mothering her younger sisters. Nicole's mother was also a hoarder and often left Nicole to care for her younger sisters and dodge CPS investigations while she worked. Her mother did not nurture her, and Nicole couldn't name what was missing in their relationship until she became a mother. While growing up, she felt more like a partner, roommate, and nanny than a daughter. One of Nicole's goals was to figure out why it was so easy for her to fall in love with abusive partners. She learned that serving her mother and being denied her own needs for the needs of others fractured her emotional growth and set her up to be a people pleaser. She was parentified. When a child is groomed to fulfill the needs of an adult, whether sexually, emotionally, or financially, it elevates that child to adult status due to all the responsibility. This is parentification. When you hear someone is an 'old soul,' or a 'little woman' or deemed 'The man of the house' at 10 years old, that child has likely been parentified. They aren't allowed to be children. Instead, they take up the slack of the adults who are supposed to be in charge. Some children are asked to do this. Some children notice the gaps in responsible adulting and take on the role all on their own. When this structure exists, these kids learn their needs do not matter. In adulthood, they can become people pleasers, doormats (domestic violence victims), or, the reverse, the CEO, the group project leader. Some angrily take what they want without permission or apology - unable or unwilling to articulate their emotions or acknowledge they have any. They can also disguise their pain with humor. These opposing personalities can attract each other and perpetuate the relationship dynamic.

Nicole desperately wanted to feel love, but, unfortunately, she had no models of healthy relationships to learn from. In her first significant relationship, she fell in love with someone who love bombed her. Love bombing is weaponizing love by being overly affectionate or showering someone with material things to manipulate another person into a relationship. It's a common tactic of narcissists. When deprived of healthy attachments and experiencing nothing but dysfunction, you may fall for love bombing and think it sincere. Nicole felt appreciated and flattered by the attention she was getting. She did not realize that the bomber was setting her up to feel dependent and obligated to him. Her mother set the stage for that. Nicole had to fight her feelings of guilt, which eventually subsided. She decided to limit her and her son's exposure to her mother's dysfunction, which had not improved. In her mid-30s Nicole decided to reparent herself. She started therapy and created a self-care routine that included self-nurturing and carefree play. She reflected on her current friendships and cut out all the unhealthy people she realized were using her. She saw that she tended to parent the people around her without reciprocal attention.

It's okay and necessary to champion your growth beyond your early dysfunctional family system and make boundaries to protect yourself. It's okay not to answer phone calls and emails or decline holiday invitations to keep yourself safe. You do not need your children to have relationships with unhealthy grandparents. Don't let guilt or denial trick you into thinking your mother is a great-grandparent and simultaneously a shitty parent to you. You must protect your kids. You must break the trauma cycle.

The shame and judgment heaped on people who have distanced themselves from destructive mothers is uncalled for and misplaced. A person should be allowed to discuss their antagonistic relationship with their mother and its effect on them without criticism. Years ago, I dated a man who shrugged off my description of my relationship with my drug-addict mother, calling me "Just one of those girls annoyed by their mother." When psychologist Dr. Laura Schlessinger's mother died, and her body wasn't found for several weeks, she and her siblings released a statement about their estrangement due to their mother's toxicity. A boss of mine at the time was disgusted by the statement, calling it cold and ungrateful. I replied, "Not everyone grew up with the loving and supporting mother you have." He thought for a moment, then shut up. Stop judging and be curious. I'm not saying to batter someone with a ton of personal questions, but don't assume the child is at fault when there's parental estrangement. We need to create spaces for people to discuss their experiences without being shamed or judged. We all applaud when the decision is made to end a toxic romantic relationship, that same latitude should be given to severing ties with dysfunctional parents.

Do you see your relationship with your mother in any of the above stories? How have you translated your mother's parenting style, or lack thereof, into your identity? Here are a few ways (this list appeared in the chapter on Fathers too) being emotionally or physically abandoned by your mother can look:

- **Low self-esteem or sense of self:** If the person who created you isn't there for you, then you feel you have no value—difficulty trusting others and yourself.
- **People Pleasing** – Diving into or staying in unhealthy relationships quickly. Doing too much for others or doing things you don't want to do so others won't leave you.
- **Relationship Issues** – Attaching too quickly to the wrong people or not attaching to anyone at all. The eternal bachelor – no one is ever good enough; the loner who sticks to themselves—feeling unworthy of anyone's love or attention. Also, choosing people who will abandon you because they are unavailable to you physically (married, live far away, entrenched in a job or hobby you can't participate in) – creates a self-fulfilling prophecy.
- **Hypersexuality:** You want love and intimacy, but since that wasn't healthily modeled for you, you choose promiscuous sex to be close to others instead of communicating intimate needs.
- **Fear of letting go** – It's hard for you to walk away from toxic jobs, toxic relationships, status symbols you can't afford to maintain.
- **Addictions and addictive behavior:** If you weren't taught healthy ways to take care of yourself when

stressed, you look for ways (usually maladaptive) to soothe.

- **Hyperarousal** - Never feeling safe, secure, or settled in anything: your identity, your home, your job, or your relationships.
- **Needing Constant Distraction** - You find being alone with yourself, your thoughts, and emotions difficult so you are always filling time and space with people, errands, activities, your phone, etc.

The following did not appear in the list for distant fathers.
- **Unrealistic Expectations of others and yourself** – When people fail or disappoint, you find forgiving nearly impossible.
- **Fear of rejection** - Initiating plans, relationships, and situations with others is difficult.
- **Diminishing reliance or need for others** - You downplay your need for others or their significance in your life.
- **Playing Small** – You're reluctant to take up space, go for your dreams and speak up.
- **Chaos** – You gravitate towards chaos. Your life is marinating in chaos. Something negative is always happening - a battle to fight, a new enemy, the latest problem to solve. You see yourself as a victim that doesn't acknowledge your part in initiating your drama.
- **Clingy** – You are excessively touchy, everyone is your best friend, and you overshare intimate details quickly.

If you recognize these traits in yourself, and you want to be in a relationship with other people you need to make healing a priority. What we don't heal we repeat.

CHAPTER 5

Siblings

Siblings are usually our first friends, teachers, and guides through our first social exchanges. They are vital in our personal development. If there's anyone in the world we're supposed to be most similar to, it's our brothers and sisters. Our identities, coping skills, wounds, and strengths are developed with our siblings. We learn how to navigate the future world by connecting daily with them. However, living with siblings can also feel like you're going through the worst kind of boot camp because our siblings can also be our first bullies, abusers, or competitors for attention and resources. Favoritism and rivals for a parent's love can create a wedge between siblings in a system controlled by adults and misunderstood by children. Also, if parents are dysfunctional, they could model bad behavior older siblings continue with younger siblings including physical, emotional, and sexual abuse. Therefore, fractures in this dynamic can be devastating when we can actually navigate life and its impact together as teammates.

Mourning sibling relationships is challenging because you're linked to them usually longer than your parents, and there isn't the same pressure to honor them. There are always expectations of closeness, and it sucks if it doesn't exist. Analyzing sibling dynamics can drive you crazy, especially when you're so different. How can we be so different when we grew up in the same house and were created by the same people? How can one sibling be a natural leader, responsible, and successful and another be a thief without ambition? For YEARS, this tripped me until I had an epiphany about my sibling dynamics. If we go beyond the surface, I don't think we're all that different from our siblings, even if one is an addict, another is self-centered and immature, while another is stable and successful. I feel all siblings have the same qualities but at varying degrees. Just like everything else in life - we're on a spectrum.

When I was a kid, my older sister and I didn't like our older brother. We'd been separated from the start because our grandparents raised him. Our grandparents were stable and successful and could shower him with stability, support, and material things that we didn't receive living with our addict mother. We didn't realize until adulthood that our anger at him was misplaced. He didn't set the wheels of inequality in motion. We were mad at him for something he didn't initiate. The adults' decisions placed a wedge in our sibling relationships that is still being mended after all these years.

Growing up, my older sister experienced more severe trauma than I did. I have to keep this in mind if I try to hold her to expectations she can't possibly meet. To heal, I dove into therapy. I had to understand my childhood, the people in it, and how all these elements played a part in who I became and how I see myself in the world. I had to dive in to move beyond.

Therapy requires trust, and that's a tall order for people who have been betrayed and hurt by the very people meant to love and protect you. It's much harder for my sister to trust due to being neglected and abused by so many people for so long. Owning our different realities reminds me that I need to be patient and compassionate as I interact with her, but these lessons have been challenging and have taken years for me to learn. This isn't to say she gets a free pass to behave with impunity. She still needs to respect my boundaries (she doesn't), understand how her behavior affects her children (she doesn't) and work towards healing herself (she does sporadically). As frustrated as I can get, I can still extend her grace, the grace she didn't receive as a little girl.

Every family has layered components, and siblings help us navigate those systems. Each sibling has a different relationship with the adults in the home and those differences need to be respected even if misunderstood - including codependency. Don't misunderstand that statement. Respecting codependency isn't endorsing it; it's acknowledging that dysfunction and unexpressed pain exist. Yes, codependency is maladaptive, but if that's what's happening in your family, dwelling on the why or its dysfunction is not helping you work with it or around it. How often have you and a sibling had different memories about the same events? If you know your sibling isn't maliciously manipulative, both of you are correct.

When our father died, my older sister was with him. I'd cut him out of my life decades before because I never felt he cared or protected us as a father should. Despite this, he and my sister remained close. She screamed at me when I didn't react emotionally to the news of his passing. She was pissed because she thought I should feel like she did - devastated. She didn't realize that I had already mourned him throughout my childhood. When he didn't intervene and take an active role in parenting us, that would have potentially stopped the abuse from our mother and her partners when he didn't come to any of my graduations or contribute to any school activities. When he allowed his new wives to dictate his involvement in our lives, I stopped seeing him as my father. My sister didn't. She accepted it all, explained it away, and held on. I didn't understand her desire to do so, but respected it. Until he died, I didn't know she didn't appreciate my desire to create a boundary between him and myself. After her anger subsided, we talked, and she said she accepted my point of view.

When a child is conceived and born, parents are either in love, stressed, financially stable, desperate, on the edge of divorce, emotionally distant, enthusiastic, loving, angry, and a host of other emotional states. A child's disposition is based on the parent's current state of mind. (An astrologer read my birth chart and told me that at the time of my birth, my parents were at a significant low point in their marriage. It makes so much sense because they divorced when I was three.) My sister witnessed our parents' love, hope, and enthusiasm. So, when they separated, I think it was more devastating to her. The fear, the uncertainty, the fights... I don't remember anything about their relationship, so when it was over, it didn't affect me the way it affected her. Be open and understand there is a spectrum of confidence, insecurity, calm, or anxiety among siblings. If you can, ask questions about your parents' emotional, financial, and psychological states when you and your siblings were born and in the early years. Be honest about how you may have benefitted in ways your siblings did not.

There is also a lot said about birth order. Psychiatrist Alfred Adleand and many other scientists worldwide have researched the potential connection between where you were born in relation to your siblings and how the order of your birth may determine your personality. Criticisms to the Birth Order Theory cannot be dismissed, considering the number of variables to try to control are virtually unlimited. Yet, due to the many conversations about the first child being responsible and most successful and the "middle" child being more problematic due to a thirst for attention, some people have either taken on these traits as their identities or the behaviors have been projected in childhood.

Tara's Sister

My sister Helen and I are only 19 months apart, so we were very close throughout childhood. I have great memories of growing up in the country and running barefoot with her, playing softball together, and taking dance classes. Helen was the one who always got all the attention because there was nothing that she was not good at. She was the star player on the softball team, the soloist at our ballet recitals, and the one that everyone in my family knew would grow up to be a lawyer because she was so smart. Her being blonde, blue-eyed, and slim was also part of her charm. She was confident and outgoing, and I was brown-haired, brown-eyed, overweight, and sometimes could be extremely shy. I remember that my Mom took us to try out for a play at the community college when we were probably ten years old or so. The play was The Wizard of Oz, and we were so excited. Helen got a part, but I did not. I remember my Mom calling the theater department and begging them to give me a part. She was able to convince them to let me in, but I was so embarrassed. I just knew that I was not supposed to be there.

My parents, my Mom especially, are hippies. They would party quite a bit when we were young, and at some point, we started to realize what pot was and where my parents kept their stash. By 7th grade, we were siphoning off our parents' stash and smoking weed. My sister and I both continued to use drugs throughout our high school years, of course increasing what drugs we were trying out and latching on to. There was a difference, though, I could stop and decided to do so soon after graduation. But, Helen, she was deep into it by then. It was not fun for me anymore, but for her, it was her life. She would start disappearing here and there for a few days. My brother knew where her dealer lived, so we would go find her and pull her out of crack houses. Sometimes with success and sometimes not. At that time, my sister had a great job (one of many). She disappeared on another binge, and her employer called my Mom concerned that something had happened to my sister. They thought that her boyfriend had done something to her. What do you say in a situation like that? Sorry, your employee/my daughter is a drug addict? I cannot count how often we would protect her from friends or employers finding out.

I started seeing Helen differently when she gave birth to my niece, Karly. Before Karly was a year old, Helen received a DUI with child endangerment charges because Karly was in the car with her when she passed out in someone's driveway. I remember the police calling me, asking me to pick up my niece. When I exited the car, the police officer told me to be calm. Now, I am a very calm person and I said, "no problem". But, when I laid eyes on my sister, I lunged for her. I was so angry, and it just boiled up in me at that moment. After that horrific incident, Helen was sober for three years. The longest that she has been sober before and since.

When we thought her addiction could not get any worse, it did. She then started using meth. This is when Helen's mental state started becoming more and more concerning. I had to make one of the hardest decisions that I have ever made, and that was to call Child Protective Services. But CPS was not able to help much because my sister would just not answer the door when they would come by. By a miracle, we were able to talk my sister into signing over my niece to me temporarily. She lived with me for several months and then my Mom and Dad for several more. Helen got clean yet again, and my niece went back to her. But then we started seeing signs of her using again and her deteriorating mental state. Through the grapevine, she heard that my partner had inherited some money that we ended up investing. Helen created a scenario in her head that there was a mass conspiracy against her. It made absolutely no sense to anyone except her. Soon, she was on a bender again. Something that small and false turned into her disappearing again. When she showed back up, she sent me hateful text messages. That's when I was done. I blocked her from any way of contacting me. I have to say that it was a huge weight lifted off me. It was a relief that I did not have to deal with her anymore.

During this time, she went to rehab. The holidays were coming up and my Mom asked me to allow Helen back in my life. It took some convincing because although I was mad at her, I didn't feel good not talking to her. I unblocked her from my phone because I love my Mom and it was important to her.

Fast forward, our relationship is pretty one-sided. I've learned that I don't have to pick up every time she calls me. It's strange to try to explain my feelings for her now. She is my sister, and I love her, but I want her out of my life as much as possible. I want her to be free of her addictions, but I am always waiting for them to creep back in.

Honestly, I have not done anything to heal from the loss of my sister. Although we are in contact with each other, I do consider it a failure because I have lost any semblance of a sisterly relationship. This is the first time that I have talked about it with anyone outside of my family. It is tough, I just put one foot in front of the other and hope for the best.

Michelle's Story

My brother is in a cult, and we don't know how to get him out. He follows this guy who tells people to kill themselves if they don't have a purpose in life. I'm scared shitless. I mean, if someone had purpose in life, it seems like being in a cult wouldn't be an attractive situation. I don't know. We don't know why he would go in one at all. Our family isn't perfect, but it isn't horrible either.

We don't know what we did or didn't do right with him. He was overly dysfunctional, too. He was always a highly sensitive person. He always seemed deeply affected by anything happening around him. He wasn't super emotional, but he always seemed unsettled. I did not think about this as we grew up. I was just a kid, too. I can only speculate now. I have no way of confirming anything since he shut us out. Honestly, now that I think about it, we weren't close growing up. I guess you could say I was the popular one. I always had friends to hang out with. I was always on the go at an event or a party. I guess he did his own thing. I assume he did. I never felt like I had to hang out with him. I feel guilty about that now. Maybe I should have asked him to hang out, asked about his goals, picked his brain about something... anything.

Now I've got nothing. I think our parents feel guilty too, my dad especially. I've never known my dad to cry about anyone or anything except my brother. I don't think we'll even know how he is unless he's dead and the cops let us know. It's weird because he already feels dead to us.

My Story

I'm one of four siblings, but my older sister and I are the closest in age. Our mother had our older brother when she was 16. I think the plan was for my grandparents to raise him until my mother got on her feet. My mother went to my grandparents to take my brother, but they wouldn't allow it. I heard there was a shotgun involved.

When my mother was 19, she married my father. My mother and father had my older sister, Casey, when our mom was 20.

I came three years later. Three years after that, their marriage was over. Our father went on to two other families, being a model stepfather to those kids, but only briefly visited Casey and me for the first few years after the divorce.

Our mother dated a series of men, each introducing a new drug or level of abuse into our lives. First was weed, then cocaine, then prescription pills. She settled on crack, which she abused for decades before drinking alcohol. She would take off for days or weeks at a time. Leaving money on a counter, and sometimes not. My older sister and I clung to each other throughout every boyfriend, drug binge, meltdown, and eviction. In my late teens, I found out our stepfather had molested my sister with our mother's permission for years. As adults, my sister told me she didn't fight off our stepfather because he threatened to rape me if my sister didn't do what he wanted. She didn't know it had already begun.

Growing up, Casey was my favorite person. She was funny, strong and resilient. She cared for, protected, cooked, did my hair, and eventually bought me my first car. By 19, she was a single mom. She decided the best leap forward for her and her son was by joining the military. She left my nephew with our grandparents and lived in Tennessee, Alaska, and Germany. While away, she'd gotten married, had another son, got divorced, and ended an engagement. When she returned to Texas, she soon became pregnant without a job or a home. She was lost and probably felt alone, but she didn't stay down long. Eventually, she became a civil servant, bought a house, got remarried, and had her third child. During this time, I moved to California, but I visited my sister and her kids each time I went home.

My sister is known for casually dropping major life bombs like you should've already known. I found lumps in my breasts and was scared. As I waited for the biopsy results, my sister called and flippantly said she'd survived breast cancer two years prior and I'd be fine. That was it. No emotion. I couldn't believe she went through that, and she told no one. She isolated herself, explained her hair loss as a style choice, and made her children keep the secret. Her explanation was - 'Why tell you? There's nothing you could do about it.'

One day, our little sister called me crying after a call with Casey. Casey was having surgery the following day to remove a tumor! WTF? How are we here again? I was pissed. Her response was, 'Why tell you? There's nothing you could do about it.' She always dropped nuggets like this, including her first relationship as a teenager. She suffered domestic violence before, during, and after her pregnancy with her first child.

At this point, she's a full-on drug addict just like our mother. She was so strong for so long, but she's exhausted now. After years in the military, financial issues, dysfunctional relationships, and miscarriages - I think it all became too much for her to carry. Especially considering all the unprocessed trauma she'd suffered in our childhood. She started choosing boyfriends over raising her children, using drugs, and getting fired and evicted... just like our mother. She was my everything, and then, she became nothing to me. It was just disappointment and rage every time I thought of her. How could she choose drugs and men over her children? She tells lies to cover up other lies. Why is she ignoring the effect our mother's choices had on us? While she is twisting in the wind, so are her children. Her kids started being embarrassed by her. CPS got involved, erratic behavior persisted, and so did the lies. She eventually became homeless, doing all kinds of things for and while on drugs... just like our mother.

My heart is broken because my sister is gone. My funny, resilient, silly sister became the topic that made my eyes roll. I cried A LOT, chose anger and pettiness instead of understanding, and tried to ignore her to relieve the pain. Eventually, YEARS later, I'm trying a new tactic - curiosity and compassion. She was emotionally neglected by the two people she was supposed to trust the most: our parents. If you can't trust your parents, trusting others, including yourself is nearly impossible. Being vulnerable isn't an option when you're always in survival mode. I had to learn to separate my sister's behavior from her heart and true intentions. I need to remember all the crap she's been through in order to cut her some slack.

My sister used to make fun of me for going to therapy. She didn't realize I HAD to go to therapy so I wouldn't repeat the cycle. I needed to learn how to function in a healthy way instead of self-soothing with substances like most of the people in our family. This year, my sister called me at 5 am the morning for my birthday. We hadn't spoken in years. We laughed, cried, and caught up for 3 hours. She was sober, in therapy, and on medication. She was honest, open, humble - vulnerable. What a fantastic gift to get a glimpse of the woman I once knew. We may never be who we used to be for each other, but I understand why she is who she is. I have to accept that and love her from a distance to protect myself and protect her from my judgment. I love her but can't let her dysfunctional behavior tamper with my peace. But, when she's sober again, I'll be there for her.

Matthew's Story

Honestly, I don't know if my brother is dead or alive. For years, when we were kids, we shared a room, played sports, and hung out with his friends. We were three years apart, but he didn't mind me tagging along. Now, I don't even know his phone number. We grew up 'country poor' like dirt roads, dirty faces, and none of the adults graduated from high school poor. He worked his way through high school and then college, paying for classes when he saved enough money—stopping when he ran out—starting again after a stretch of working. He didn't know most kids get loans to attend because he was the first in our family to graduate high school and go to college. He went along this way for several years until he graduated.

When he first left for school, he would visit as often as possible. Within two years, he came home less and less, and his trips became shorter and shorter. I assumed it was because he needed to go back so he wouldn't get fired from a job. He was always strapped for cash because our folks couldn't afford to help him out. Eventually, his trips stopped altogether. When he came back for our dad's funeral, he didn't even look like he came from our family. Everything was different, the way he dressed and talked. He even walked different. He stood out like a sore thumb. I asked how he'd been doing, what he'd been up to. He said he was engaged to a girl from New York. I wondered why he didn't bring her, and he said she was at a friend's wedding up there. I didn't even know he wanted to live in New York. He didn't stay long but seemed to complain about everything while there. The dirt roads, old one-story buildings, lack of foods he now liked. I asked when we'd meet his girl, but he never gave me a real answer. When he left, I felt I'd never see him again. I was right. After a while of unanswered calls and texts I Googled him. I saw the wedding announcement that he'd married that girl. He didn't invite any of us. I guess he was embarrassed by us. I could find his number if I really tried but I'm afraid of being rejected. But, I miss him and hope he knows I still love him.

I think it's helpful to allow yourself to feel everything you can about your sibling: pride, sadness, jealousy, anger, disappointment, and more. Take note of your reactions and responses to their behavior, your parents' decisions, and unpredictable life events that affected both of you. As an adult, remember old situations will color your current relationship because you may remember things differently. Apologize when you feel it necessary. Ask for clarification, validation and apologies if you when appropriate. Remind yourself that they will most likely see the same situations differently because of their own perspectives. If reunification is the goal, choose your battles. Don't fight about details. Both of you are right and can respect each other's point of view. And choose which hill to die on. To reach a greater understanding and bond, get past small details by agreeing to disagree. If the big picture includes closeness, you must let some stuff go. If you can't agree to disagree respectfully, maybe you need to walk away.

> *"When we avoid difficult conversations, we trade short-term comfort for long-term dysfunction."*
> *- Peter Bromberg*

If you're debating whether to cut ties, you get to decide where, when, and how this happens or if it happens at all. Keep in mind that you may be the sibling that's confronted. You may be the sibling seen as "the issue". Try to write down your thoughts and emotions before you talk so you can process them on your own and then again with your sibling. Remember, you can create boundaries for these conversations. You can decide whether a phone call, email or face-to-face works best for you. If your sibling is a healthy and reasonable person, negotiate terms because they deserve to be comfortable as well. You can limit your discussions to specific topics or a time range and place rules on communication, such as no cursing, yelling or name-calling.

Creating a family genogram can be an enlightening and bonding experience between siblings. Genograms look like the family trees we made as kids but go far beyond who married who and had which children. It tracks relationships and behaviors therefore, you can see patterns. You can see patterns in relationships, lengths of commitments, estrangements, anything you want as long as you have the information. It helps you acknowledge the past, which puts context to the present, and helps prepare for the future. When you confront these things and change how you communicate and interact with others, you actively break generational curses. Have the guts to go inside your family history to heal yourself, understand and forgive others, and release pain. Externalizing our healing is dismissive and keeps harmful and unhealthy patterns alive. Dumping your hurt on others is destructive. The saying, "Hurt people hurt people," comes from this. Take the time to map the relationship history of your parents, grand, great-grandparents, aunts, uncles, and cousins. It'll be an enlightening experience that can release shame that never belonged to you. Also, remember that healed people heal people. Your siblings may not grow beyond their traumas. That doesn't stop you from maintaining relationships with their children and helping them move beyond their dysfunctional parents.

Working with Clients

It can be hard to fathom how siblings who grow up in the same household at the same time with the same parents can make very different choices and lead very different lives. One way to conceptualize this is to consider your primary caregivers. Traditionally they are your parents but sometimes it's extended family: grandparents, aunts, uncles or step-parents or foster families and even group homes. Siblings raised in the same home, by the same people will be different because they are being parented by people navigating all of life's ups and downs while raising the kids. If caregivers are in love, kids feel it. If caregivers are anxious about money, kids feel it (and that forms their relationship with money). If caregivers feel unhappy in some way, shape or form, kids feel it. So, if your parents are gainfully employed and in love when you are little you'll see the world and yourself in a certain way. But, let's say one loses their job, there's a major health issue, the family loses all their money or one parent is caught cheating - each child will feel the disruption at their own developmental level and internalize or externalize the emotions of their environment. That may mean acting out or shutting down and/or everything in between.

Sarah

Sarah came to me to work on her anxiety. Everything frightened her to the point that she rarely left her home. I eventually learned about her siblings and both are addicts. Sarah tried to help both, stoking her codependent tendencies. They said they wanted better lives but made no effort to effect change. She felt responsible for them because they grew up together. And, because she was feeling better, she wanted them to be well, too. Some siblings report experiencing survivor's guilt if their lives are healthier than their brothers or sisters. She expressed this and didn't want them to hurt anymore because her pain was decreasing, and she wanted them to experience relief also. As she improved her self-care and learned positive coping skills, they casually laced conversations with passive suicidal ideation. It's like she was on a seesaw. When she inserted conversations with joy and achievement, they lay on the doom and gloom. She had to create boundaries with each so they wouldn't drag her back down. She needed to see them change or at least respect her changes if their relationships were to continue in a way that's healthy for her.

I suggested she use a Dialectical Behavioral Therapy skill called D.E.A.R.M.A.N. DBT is an evidence-based therapeutic model that helps people with intense emotions that cause issues in their relationships with others and themselves. It's also proven to help people with suicidal and self-harm behaviors. (These terms are separate because engaging in self-harm does not necessarily mean someone is suicidal). DBT helps people accept that they can experience opposing emotions simultaneously yet rein them in so they aren't in control of you. It helps people to stop allowing their feelings to make decisions for them.

D.E.A.R.M.A.N. is a method of scripting a conversation to ask someone to change something for you or, more pointedly, change behavior in a specific way. It's mutually beneficial and allows for negotiation. This method can be used with everyone from a partner to a co-worker, your mother or friend. From returning a shirt to a store, asking someone to adjust their tone of voice, or asking for repayment of a loan. If it's difficult for you to initiate a conversation, use this method. Don't rehearse this in your head, then dive in expecting to knock it out of the park the first time you try it. Start small by practicing this in a situation with low significance - a store clerk or a server. Writing it out first helps you process the problem and will decrease any strong emotions you may have in the matter before you talk.

Describe the situation using the facts only. No opinions and refrain from discussing your emotional state. Unfortunately, most people are uncomfortable with their emotions, which means they're probably even more uncomfortable with your emotions. Please don't stop the conversation before it starts by heaving your feelings on them first. Some get defensive and blast everything you're trying to say because they feel attacked or shamed. Also, you want to ensure you are on the same page about a situation's facts before asking for someone to change something. For example, "I washed the dishes last night. On Sunday, we agreed that you would wash the dishes after dinner every day this week by 9 pm. What do you remember?" Starting with the facts helps to insure you and the other person are on the same page about the facts of a situation before you ask them to change something.

Emotion. This is the point where you tell the other person how their behavior or the situation makes you feel. This will help the other person understand how significant the situation is to you. Share whether you are scared, disappointed, or angry. Be sure not to attack the other person or slip into victim-mode. Be honest and do not exaggerate.

Assert. This is the point where you articulate the change you want someone to make for you. "I need you to do the chores we agreed upon and do them when we decided they should be done. I will do the same." "I want you to use a calm tone when asking me to do something. Loud voices tend to shut me down." "I need you to return with a rare steak. I didn't order well-done."

Reinforce – This is where you share how the change the other person makes will benefit them too. It incentivizes the change. For example, "When you do the dishes by 9pm, the kitchen is clean when we make breakfast in the morning."

Mindful - Be present as the exchange is unfolding. Don't get distracted by other unresolved issues the other party can lob your way. When this happens, validate them, promise to address their concerns/issues later, and then return to the original problem. Don't get distracted and taken off course, or if you do, reevaluate. If you don't, the issue will remain unchanged but add to the mountain of unresolved problems. So many people get stuck in this loop and nothing ever gets fixed. Stay focused and tackle each issue.

Act Confident during your delivery. Establish and maintain eye contact, carry a strong posture, and be aware of your tone of voice. People are more willing to accommodate your requests when they see you're confident while asking for what you want.

Negotiate - When you need something from someone, they'll be more likely to accommodate you by getting something in return, even if it's merely understanding their point of view. Does the other party have ideas on how they can make your request happen easier for them? Maybe not a full discount but 50% off. Perhaps they wash, and you dry the dishes. Maybe you get half of your loan repaid today then the remaining amount in 30 days. This is where their input is respected, heard, and discussed to meet your needs.

Victoria

My client Victoria has an older brother who she considers "one of the angriest people in the world." She isn't sure why. She feels something big happened to him but doesn't know what or when. "I'm clueless. When we were growing up he had no friends. He was always a loner. Back then, it wasn't that big of a deal but now, those are the men that usually cause mass shootings. I hate to think about him that way but I do wonder if he's capable of it." When Victoria was young, she said she repeatedly asked her parents questions about why her brother acted the way he did. He pushed her around, skipped school, and failed classes. She thinks they were lenient and allowed him to get away with "murder" being rude and disrespectful to all of them without reprimand. "I had to make straight As but they never punished him or pressured him the way they did me. I think they felt guilty about something they either did to him or didn't do for him. It's a big mystery!"

"Over the years I tried to get close to him many times. Invite him places, strike up conversations but I was shut down every time. I've stopped bringing it up to our parents because they just brush it off or say I'm too nosey or pushy. They're ignoring my needs the way they probably ignored his when we were younger. They're getting older and I don't want to be in this alone. I want my brother. I wish I knew why he was so closed off. I guess I have to let him go but I don't want to. I want my brother in my life in a real way."

Victoria, a naturally curious person, has had to get comfortable being uncomfortable with a potential family secret. Chances are she'll never know if something happened to her brother. "When he got a girlfriend, we were all shocked. She's really kind but kind of clueless yet co-dependent. She protects him, shields him. They got married because I don't think he had the energy to try to date anyone else. I don't know her well because they moved across the country right after getting married. I think she caters to him and his crappy personality even over their kids. I feel so sorry for their kids, especially their oldest son. He doesn't know his father shouldn't be his role model because he's so damaged. It's like the blind leading the blind over there. We see them about once a year during the holidays. Even them showing up seems performative because none of us are particularly warm to each other. I sense the anger brewing inside my nephew and it scares me."

Victoria has hesitated starting her own family for fear of replicating the shallow connection between her immediate family members. She says she did a deep dive into her own identity, her chosen identity to understand her hypervigilance may come in handy because she doesn't want what she grew up in. "I think they want me to write everything off and just move on. I can't do that. If something happened to him, what if something happened to me and I just don't remember? I want kids but I don't want to pass on something negative to them."

Being honest about your situation can help decrease or eliminate unnecessary frustration. As painful as it was to stop acknowledging her brother's behavior and how it didn't align with her own, it was necessary so she could move on. Whatever transpired between him and her parents is between him and her parents. Only they will decide if she is made aware of the cause between their dysfunctional dynamics. Although her family situation has not been ideal, she has a basis for what she doesn't want for the family she creates. She continues in therapy to learn respectful communication skills, radical acceptance and forgiveness. She's also learned that people heal at their own pace, in their own time IF they choose to heal at all.

Addiction can cause the most ugly behavior. I think one of the most disrespectful acts someone can do to someone else is manipulation. Addicts will do and say anything to get a fix including lying and using people they love. You have to be steeped in truth and self-protection to get through this. The person you're dealing with now isn't the person you used to know. Don't fall for the 'I thought you loved me' tugs at your heart strings. Boundaries will help keep further erosion of your relationship at bay.

Whether addiction or estrangement is the issue, spend time remembering all the good times. Your sibling is more than their current behavior. Think about all of their skills, talents and good qualities. I like to think of each life as a quilt and each life event is a square on our quilt. We should not be reduced to our worst moments. None of us are only our worst moments. We have so many sides to us, so much to offer, so much that plays a part in who we are right now. When you reflect on your siblings, think about their humor, intelligence, soccer or painting skills, gorgeous brown eyes. My sister has the mind of a mathematician. She's extremely resourceful and one of the funniest people you'll ever meet. And her handwriting is more beautiful than the most elegant calligraphy. She can also cook like a Michelin-starred chef.

CHAPTER 6

Children

"Grief is like living two lives. One is where you pretend that everything is alright, and the other is where your heart silently screams in pain."
- D.H. Lawrence

Outside of the "Whoops! We'll figure it out!" parenting path, deciding if you will raise a child is the single most significant decision you will ever make. A child in your care will positively or negatively impact the world depending on their decisions... and yours. Unlike apartments, partnerships, or jobs, you cannot walk away from parenting without severe devastation. Being a present parent doesn't mean perfection by any means, but being absent means a considerable loss that must be grieved so you don't perpetuate pain. In no way, shape, or form am I endorsing having an unhealthy parent in a child's life is better than their absence - a physical presence is not enough. Some parents leave (even by suicide) because they think that's the best thing for their child. Just know a kid is not emotionally or psychologically mature enough to understand this. Neglect is more detrimental than you realize.

Regardless of whether you've expressed your contentment with just having 10 fingers and ten toes, there are expectations that come with having a baby. Some would like to see a carbon copy of themselves to fit the "Jr." title or "Mini Me" status. Some would love to see their beauty, athleticism or creative prowess shine through their children. Sometimes, the expectations are for the parents. (Unfortunately, there are still men and women who try to trap partners via pregnancy.) Looks, height, intelligence, confidence, popularity... Perhaps the only person who could parent without expectations would be the Dalai Lama. BTW, did he ever knock anyone up? If so, how's that kid doing?

Raising children is an ever-fluctuating mix of reward, sacrifice, and WTF. Most potential parents would like to enter this phase naturally. Sperm + Egg = Healthy Baby in 9ish months. But what if that combo doesn't prove productive? What if you can't find a partner to do it with? What if you don't want a partner at all? What if the kid you birth has special needs? What if the kid you foster or adopt has an undiagnosed mental illness? Any of the above combinations and many more iterations of parenthood are lovely, worthy, valid, sometimes scary, and, at times, tragic.

When a baby arrives, there's lots of diaper changing, feeding, and teaching. And, as the child grows, life throws many unexpected monkey wrenches at you, including medical issues, academic highs, and lows, falling in and out of love, navigating relationships, and, unfortunately, traumatic events. Your biological child will grow and throw you many surprises. Fostering and adopting a child will bring you the same challenges and can take the job of parenting to an entirely different level. These kiddos have experienced trauma earlier than most, and the effects can be with them for their lifetimes and yours.

Kids in the foster care system suffer their first relational traumas via dysfunctional parental behavior, which can shift to separation trauma for many regardless of whether or not a child was willingly relinquished. Many kids are removed from dangerous homes, but that doesn't mean they live happily ever after. The adults (potential foster parents, case workers, the courts, etc.) know removing a child is usually the safest path, but little kids don't understand what's happening. All they grasp is that they live with relatives one minute, and the next minute they're with strangers. Everyone around them knows what is happening and why, EXCEPT the kid at the center of the chaos. Allow space for your children to have opinions not in line with your own. Adolescence is challenging for kids in the healthiest homes; imagine trying to figure out who you are while living with strangers, regardless of how well-meaning they are.

Adopting an older child takes patience and balls of steel because your knowledge of the child's history is usually a mystery. Social services do their best to furnish as much information as possible, but you never know what could lie ahead regarding mental and genetic health issues.

Regardless of how your child comes into your life, it would help if you let go of any fantasy scenarios you may have in mind. Parent the child you have, not the child you wish you had. Realistic expectations are critical for a child to thrive in being who they are meant to be. In this next chapter you'll learn about the triumphs and agony parents felt while coming to terms with their children's challenges. You may be managing the feelings and issues of raising a child with severe mental and physical illnesses with style and grace. But what if you don't have access to all the resources that can make your situation easier? What if you don't have the money, social support, insurance, or time to really dive into finding solutions for what ails your child? That can be highly stressful and create resentment.

Diana adopted her adolescent daughter, Melissa, out of foster care. Diana was aware her child had experienced significant trauma, leading to her removal from her parents at five. However, the depth of her child's trauma was unknown. It would soon be discovered and take their little family on a roller-coaster ride of 911 calls, therapists, psychiatric hospitals, court appearances, and financial instability.

Diana and Melissa's Story

When adopting a child, you fill out a questionnaire where there are things you can say that are basically deal breakers, things that you know you can't parent. It goes beyond race and medical needs. When you adopt an older child, there's an understanding that they usually have experienced several traumas, which can manifest in several ways. So, the things that you say for sure you can't handle are sometimes things that you end up handling. Those things for me included, 'Oh, my God! I just can't deal if they grab and spread their feces on my door or the walls' or other stuff like that. Although that seemed pretty hard to imagine dealing with regularly, the symptoms of RAD - Reactive Attachment Disorder are a whole other ball game. And the predatory, hyper-sexualized behavior that kids could experience and perpetuate. I don't even know if I got that far. I thought if there was a chance that there was something I just couldn't parent, flying poop was my biggest deal breaker.

In the introduction process, you go through several stages, and you are introduced to LOTS of kids. You get to know their past and try to assess whether you would be a good match. You imagine what your future as a family would or could look like. There's a social worker that represents the child, and then the parent or parents have a social worker that represents their interests. They have several meetings, then, there's the introduction of the prospective adoptive parents to the child. When you're introduced at this stage, it's "mommy," and it's, "I love you", and it's "forever."

I never studied this and had no idea if this was a good plan or not. And, I don't know how different our particular story is from other family's realities but I've always known that Melissa was supposed to be in my life. She was sent from God but I questioned it a lot. I asked God for signs all along the way. If this was what I was supposed to be doing. And every time, I felt in my heart that he responded that this was exactly what I was supposed to be doing and to keep putting one foot in front of the other. But, as the problems came, they never looked like what I wanted them to look like. I really struggled in ways that I didn't expect to. And then I didn't struggle in ways that I did expect to. The bottom line was she didn't have a home and needed a family. I can do this. That child has been through the wringer.

If I had gotten a child whose mom was in jail for a short time, I would have felt guilty and felt like I had broken up that family by adopting the child. And I expected to have a child brought into my life that looked nothing like me. I didn't expect the child to be white and for the child to be sort of a classic beauty. Nobody's ever questioned the legitimacy of our family because my kid looks like me. What has come into question is, am I really crazy, because she's really crazy. That has been the struggle, hoping that I'm not bringing more insanity.

Our life is not like a little anxiety, a little depression or that sort of age-appropriate kid behavior for someone in a basic midlife crisis, but the whole abuse, shame, and triggers and, and. I've never parented before so everything is foreign to me. I don't know if I am hurting her, and that's why she's being so reactive, and why is she so wholly unable to do the basic things in life. Most of the kids that are up for adoption in this day and age means there really are some serious mental health hurdles that the adoptive family should be prepared to handle and they're incredibly expensive. The specialists are ridiculous and especially expensive when you must see them a lot to learn how to approach things. You need to take care of yourself and supplement so many parts of your life with support to be fully present. There's a drive to make a dent in the lack of trust and the lack of stability that they've experienced thus far. It's a tall order.

A priest told me, 'You can only do what you can do'. I think many people are initially fueled by this idea that you can save somebody and be something more than just a human being who loves that person. Whether God puts that in you, you ask for it, or you recognize it as your destiny, I have to love someone unconditionally and entirely throughout their life, no matter what they do.

There are adjustments along the way that you have to make accordingly - big ones, especially if they don't know what love is. And if they only recognize intimacy when it is harmful and abusive and it has secrets and pacts and bonds. Understanding the ways of relating better, not just unhealthy but violent and destructive, self-destructive, and destructive of anyone or anything around them. It is sort of this idea that you're more connected because you've made it through some bloody, bloody, bloody experiences together. And conversely, talking about those experiences and sharing them with a therapist or other people has a way of diluting that bond or, worse, creating a trauma bond.

When you attempt to create intimacy with somebody young, with all those terrible experiences, that's all they have. They have had everything stolen from them: their innocence and their security, their belief in themselves, their perception of the world, and their knowledge of love, life, and beauty. Unfortunately, those experiences can become the blueprint for relationships. I used to say that Melissa was going from candy bar to candy bar. Those distractions are her life. The time between those candy bars was just her search for the following candy bar and her turning to me for that.

When I first started, I was just entirely ill-equipped to handle her level of need. Several times, we had these candid moments. The one I'll never forget included a massive meltdown that she had and I don't know what triggered it. Usually, it was just getting the word "no" to something, anything. Hearing "no" would send her into a complete and utter meltdown. I was talking to her either in or after one of these experiences. She said, 'I don't know what is real.' I said, "I'm real. Hold on to me." I reached out my hand, and she grabbed it. And it's almost as if it's been that simple ever since. There wasn't going to be a lot of back and forth about her being able to explain to me what she needed as you would expect from a typical 11 or 12-year-old. She wasn't going to be able to navigate things or help me the way that I helped my family when I was 11 and 12 years old. She was just going to hold on mostly and drag her feet because that's the best she could do. That was the point that I realized that despite how much I am providing for Melissa (counseling, stability, understanding, probably the best school experience she's ever had and living in a prime neighborhood that happened to be right next to that school), her contributions and involvement would be minor. We were in a wonderful community where she knew the priests at our church. She had developed a good relationship with my parents. And it was still not enough. It was just not enough.

I had done everything I could. I had bought everything I could think of. I had engaged every resource I could think of, and she was just getting older but not better. At 13, the hormones kicked in. I kept thinking that this time was critical. If she got help right now, during this crucial growth time she could be stronger when she was older. And I could somehow make up for this time that I devoted to her, but it was never enough. At that stress level, it was terrifying to think that this was what my future would be - not just taking care of her but being taken down by her. I worry that we are going to be living on the street and that we are going to be unable to make it because I can't. What if there wasn't a hospital or if there wasn't enough medication? Nothing seemed like enough. There are a lot of holes in her care that a full-time residential facility needed to provide. So at one point I said to her, "Do you need help? Do you need more help?" and, in a very honest moment, she said, 'Yes, I do.'

So what happens is that you go to the emergency room, because there's no reason not to. There's no other way to do it. You go to the emergency room, and then you're admitted to the psychiatric department. They ask a lot of questions and run some tests, and it's a whole process. Then, you think that you're at the end. And every time you're in the hospital, you think you're at this point where you're no longer scared and it will be manageable. But it's just not manageable. At least it wasn't for me. Then she's admitted again. And, I must tell you, it wasn't manageable then because the system is so broken. The facilities where she received care for the first several years didn't provide her with the care that she needed, the specific care that she needed. It was more punitive than rehabilitative. It was not therapeutic. It was to keep them from not hurting themselves or each other. There is a lot of isolation. And we've all heard what prolonged isolation does to people.

I found that each place had these techniques and things that they would teach her, but it would just become something that she would memorize. She wasn't understanding, learning, or growing, which was terrifying to me. I'm not sure I've ever said that. That was terrifying to me, because I was just witnessing it. I wasn't feeling it myself. I was witnessing her lack of medical care, bluntly. With anybody's child, it would have been difficult to watch. If it was a medical condition that would be understandable, like she was bleeding or she had a broken leg. I think it would have been so much easier to explain the pain of watching it. But, watching things happen to a child that you now love is rough. More than that, because you know, you can love many people and she's supposed to be my future. Watching a very delicate girl not be treated when they so desperately need it. You just don't wish that on anybody. Nobody. Mental health needs to be treated and not just managed.

I think that the only reason I can talk about it easily right now is because it's over. I feel like she's finally getting the care that she's needed and it's not with me. She's been in residential facilities for the last 3 years due to her mental health. I think that because I stopped trying to reunify with her, there was an understanding that she needs a lot more support than she is getting with outpatient services and at home with me.

So, the system is set up so that if there's a parent family that is deemed healthy, reliable, capable, they put the expectations on the family, whether those expectations are realistic or not. And in some ways, that makes total sense. But, for our family that did not make any sense at all. To just kick the can down the road. Knowing that her mental illness was based on trauma and was not going anywhere. She was not being reached and she was not getting the attention and the care that she needed. And, at some point, she's going to be 18 and then she's going to be given back to me.

When I was in college, there was a Shakespeare professor in my school, and he had the most enormous ego you've ever seen. He was also really good-looking, so it made sense, sort of. He was known for doing the same thing to every single student. He would give you a terrible grade when you first started, then a really good grade at the end. It was all about him. It's all about his ego and him wanting to be able to introduce Shakespeare to you. So I felt like that's where I was with that teacher. And I felt like this was not all about Melissa. It was not just about this child and any kind of individuality. Anything could work for regular kids; kids that hadn't been through the same kind of trauma. These kids need to do basic things like exercise, handling hygiene, nutrition, studying, and playing. None of that was a focus and that was really a rude awakening for me. It was all about survival. That's not what I'd signed up for or was this some sort of experiment? It was a lot like drinking from a firehouse.

My thought was, 'Let me be great for this kid.' And then all of a sudden, what was happening was, the good stuff was torturing that same kid... and I had to watch. At the same time, I had to go to court and deal with all kinds of people who wanted to know all sorts of things about MY mental health. Even asking sexual questions about me, in terms of my interests sexually, my romantic pursuits, and how much money I made. They required that I go into therapy. All of these questions and conversations are anxiety-inducing. I was very anxious about my future. And I was mourning the loss of not having the traditional motherhood experience that I wanted, which I had to dilute.

I had delusions that parenthood was going to feel a lot like a traditional mother/daughter relationship or like what I saw my friends' families look like. I quickly realized that this was not going to be like "Growing Pains", "Webster," or "Diff'rent Strokes" - tv families that took in kids whose only problems were trivial: sharing a bedroom with a new sibling, explaining algebra homework and reminding them to take out the trash or make their bed. And, of course, everyone gets along at the end of an episode, and it's all wrapped up in a bow at the dinner table, where everyone smiles and immediately forgives each other. I had to mourn that again, too because by my early 40s, I had to acknowledge that any iteration of that would not be my life. Adopting an 11-year-old girl out of foster care became a stark reality check. It sort of hit me upside my head. My kid had gone through a lot in her life, but those traumatic situations are not directly affecting our lives. Things affecting her are seeing a ladybug and not knowing how gentle to be—

having to ride in a carpool and wait for other kids. Not being able to get more than one dessert a day. No one knew what would throw her into a full on meltdown at any given moment. That was when I realized I could no longer post about this on social media.

Her biological family was so violent that they were put in jail for what they had done to her. It became very dangerous to put anything online that had to do with me or us. There were no pictures of her, no information about where we lived or what fun things we are doing. How would I live this fantasy parenting lifestyle without proving it on social media??? It was not going to happen. A couple of times I actually just took down my social media accounts because I became so scared of what her family could do when they got out of jail. At every turn, I became very concerned about whether we were safe or not. I'm trying to learn all of this, having never been in a situation like this before. It's like learning to fly a plane while you're already flying the plane.

Where we are now is that she is getting the care that she needs. It's not like a broken leg. There's no specific prognosis like a 'She'll be healed in 4-6 weeks' kind of thing. We are years into this, and it's still not really clear what she is ever going to be capable of in terms of self-sufficiency. She loves the promise I can keep, which is unconditional love. This story isn't over by a longshot. I'm curious about who she's going to grow up to be. It's been five years, and it feels like 500 years, but that is life. That is our life. All kinds of things that have happened have been unexpected. Losing a job, quitting a job, the pandemic... all of these things have only made things more challenging. I have to come to terms with the fact that I can only do what I can do. I'm not God, and I can't 'fix' her. She's not broken. I can't be her doctor. I can't be her therapist. I can't be her best friend. I can only be her mom, and I can love her.

You can feel the love in Diana's words. Like any good parent, she changed her life in order to create a safe and nurturing environment for her child. Diana had visions of school field trips, camping, first loves and teaching her daughter how to cook and garden. What she wanted was not a fairytale, it was hope. What she could give was solid, loving kindness but her daughter's wounds were too deep to handle on her own. What if she dismissed her child's cries for help? She would have delayed her healing and possibly assumed the love she gave to her daughter was inadequate. As painful as it was, Diana had to acknowledge love can't heal everything. At one stage Diana would repeatedly say, "This isn't mothering. This isn't parenting." Her dashed hopes of a "normal family" were dashed with every therapy appointment, school meeting, psychiatrist consultation, etc. "This IS parenting." I'd proclaim. It never looks like you think it will. Besides, all she'd experienced I'd witnessed firsthand as a therapist working with families. Parents who are biologically connected to their children experience the exact same struggles, grief, fear and frustration as adoptive and foster parents.

Diana decided to do a deep dive into herself in order to release the expectations she had for herself and her child. She had to go back to where her dreams of parenthood were born and process why specific dreams had taken root. She had to exorcize them from her head and heart and make open space for the unknown. She had to parent the child she had, not the one in her dreams. She had to allow herself to be angry at herself, her daughter, her parents and at God. She felt duped and her ego was bruised because she'd taken on a challenge she wasn't able to conquer. She had to acknowledge her loneliness. She was doing the toughest job in the world all alone and feared she'd never find someone to love her and her daughter. She had to allow herself to feel envious of other mothers who, at least on the outside, look as if they have it all figured out. She had to admit her daughter scared her. She had to admit her daughter most likely won't improve to a point of self-sufficiency.

When some parents are expecting children they can fantasize about their futures as professional athletes, doctors, artists or world leaders. Some envision their 'Mini Me' as a carbon copy of themselves or a better version of themselves living a pain-less and problem-free affluent lifestyle. Expectations run extremely high and can be loaded with judgment, hope, criticism and anxiety.

If you've felt this way, take time to look inside and just sit with the feelings, even the ones you can't quite identify. Own it all WITHOUT JUDGMENT or shame. What has your parenting experience been like? Have you felt isolated, jealous, angry, judged? What was your childhood like with your parents or caregivers? What was amazing? What hurt? Our experiences have to be processed so the good stuff is replicated and the hurtful things aren't perpetuated throughout your family.

Diana's dreams weren't extravagant. She just wanted to be a safe place for a child. She wanted to express love to her child by doing basic normal healthy things. Diana had to modify her parenting dream in order to show up in ways that her child needed and not necessarily how she wanted. She had to start with the basics even though 11 years old is an age where the "basics" have been mastered by the average child. Diana experienced resentment, disappointment, anger, regret and hope-lessness BUT every time she lost hope, it would eventually come back around. She was determined to not give up on this little human the way others had. Reminding herself of her commitment helps her regain hope every time she loses it.

How would you feel in Diana's shoes? If you're in a similar situation, how do you feel? What have you allowed yourself to admit? How have you adjusted expectations for what you hoped for?

Allison and Kyle's Story

My son was brought into the world on a hot summer day in July screaming at the top of his lungs. I don't think he stopped screaming for 6 weeks. As a first-time mom, I had no idea what to expect. I do know that he could not tolerate lying flat on his back. He would startle and scream, so none of that "back to sleep" business for him. I slept with him on my stomach in a recliner until he was able to roll over and we discovered our greatest gift: the swing. He lived in his swing with the setting on high. I thought my baby would fly out across our living room because it was going back and forth so fast. But, instead, he finally slept.

Looking back now I know this was sensory feedback that comforted him. He needed to be squeezed or rocked all the time. One thing that always comforted him was music so we could play classical music and my child would calm down. Baby Mozart.... BEST INVENTION EVER. I now know that my son was born Autistic. It wasn't a vaccine; it wasn't anything else, and trust me I've tried to figure it out. He was born this way.

As time went on, he met all of the physical milestones: crawling, walking, but not talking. He would never reach out and grab something. I would explain this away. *I know my baby so well, he does not have to ask for anything. We have a schedule, I just get it for him.* SO MUCH DENIAL. When it was time to introduce solid food to my son he would gag and vomit. Doctors would tell us, "When he gets hungry enough, he will eat". The worst advice ever..... I got him an ice cream cake for his first birthday because I thought, *Ice Cream is smooth. He'll taste it and he will love it.* To be honest it was also because I needed that picture of my son with the messy face loving his birthday cake. After he projectile vomited his ice cream cake at me on video, I thought okay, I'm a terrible mother, shoving this ice cream cake down his throat. It was a lesson learned. So many more to come. This was 2001. Autism had not entered my thoughts.

I had so many excuses as to why he did things "differently." He would be evaluated by doctors and they would say *"look at how affectionate he is, look at how he smiles and loves you and hugs you, he hugs everyone, he loves to be around people, that's not Autism"*, best news I've heard all day... more fuel for my denial. He would get ear infection after ear infection, this would explain why he was language delayed, *"his ears are always clogged so he can't hear properly"* it was one of my best excuses. I would bring him to Gymboree classes hoping to get him to play with the other kids and he loved the other kids enough to greet them, then go off to his corner, line up his toys or find a spinning toy that would occupy him the entire time. He was fascinated by handles, just flipping them back and forth could occupy him for hours. I would discourage this, taking him away from doing this repetitive action which brought him joy and fascination because, it was strange and if I keep stopping him maybe he won't want to do it anymore and he will go play with the other kids. Again nope.

Test after test, evaluation after evaluation - Finally, when my son was 7 years old, he was diagnosed with Autism PDD-NOS. As a diagnosis, it doesn't exist anymore, not it's just called Autism Spectrum Disorder. This is a late diagnosis today, if he was born even 5 years later, he would have been diagnosed earlier and had more intervention. My husband and I like to 'joke' that everything is available 2 years after we don't need it anymore. I would drive my son 50 miles each way to feeding therapy in order to teach him how to chew and swallow solid food, because there was nothing around that offered this. He was still on baby food at age 6-7 years old. Now these places are everywhere and feeding difficulties are an accepted symptom of

Autism. But, just wait he'll eat when he gets hungry was the advice from our doctors.

He went through school, had few friends and wasn't invited to many birthday parties as most children are. This weighed on me heavily. His birthday parties are family parties because we did not have friends to invite. Or the more likely scenario, I was afraid that no one would show up. He would have a few friends and seemed to be happy but his mother worried constantly and his father planned. I'm lucky that I married someone who balances me perfectly, because for all my theatrics he is level-headed and meticulous.

Why us? That was the question that I asked over and over. I felt sorry for my son, felt sorry for myself. In the 3rd grade, we had an outside psychologist observe him in school for the day and they reported to me: He has no friends, spends his time alone and I quote "It's quite sad really". I'll never forget that. But then I noticed, he didn't care. My husband, again, always the voice of reason in my unreasonable-ness, said look at him, he seems perfectly fine, he doesn't seem to mind. I'd ask him if he was ever bullied at school and he would say "no mom, I'd never let that happen" but in the back of my mind I wondered "would he even know if he was being bullied." I reconciled that if he didn't know and wasn't hurt then he was okay. He was perfectly happy spending time on his own, without people bothering him. But I was unhappy. I thought, kids need friends, they play soccer and other sports (which was a disaster) but not my child. He must feel so left out. But the weird thing is, he didn't, it was me. I felt cheated. Cheated of the life I'd always envisioned. Yes, I'm selfish and vain and I cared what others thought. I blamed myself. I threw the biggest pity parties on the planet. But one day I read "Welcome to Holland", a well-known essay written by Emily Perl Kingsley. It started to wake me up. It's said in short, you can plan and envision what you think your life is going to be, but when it doesn't happen, don't mourn, because you will miss the beautiful journey you are meant for all along. I didn't want to miss it anymore. I won't say that I don't have my days, but that was the beginning of a change in my perspective.

My son will be 20 years old in a few weeks. He has graduated high school (with a better GPA than me I might add). He went to prom, has a girlfriend and this week he will start his first job. He's not going off to college, living in the dorms and going to parties, but who cares. I worry about him every day; we still have so many questions about his future and what will happen to him. Will he be able to live on his own? I don't know. Will he ever drive a car? I don't know. I know we are trying. Will he have a career and a home and a spouse with kids? I don't know. But, if you would have asked me 15 years ago if he would have accomplished some of the things he has already done, I would have said you are crazy. I will never count this kid out; he has proven my preconceived notions wrong too many times.

One thing I do know is: I can't die, it's a lot of pressure to put on a mother, but it is what it is. I just can't die and leave him. This is my greatest fear, leaving my son to fend for himself in this world. So, since 'never dying' does not seem to be an option right now, I have to leave him with the services and tools to make it without me. I don't know how we will get there, but that's the journey ahead. Our terrifying, beautiful, heartbreaking, stressful and wondrous journey ahead. So, here's to immortality and my kid!"

I appreciate how Allison was able to be honest about her dance with denial. It would be appropriate to assume she felt some anger and embarrassment for his delayed diagnosis and treatment. She doesn't beat herself up about it anymore because guilt is wasted energy. She knows now. Besides, medical doctors and other professionals with PhDs missed the diagnosis without feeling embarrassed or ashamed. It doesn't matter if you've given birth to your little person, you're not going to know everything about your kid or what can 'fix' them. It is what it is. Only assholes will judge you for not knowing something an average person wouldn't know. Better late than never is a stance you could adopt in this scenario.

In therapeutic circles we use the phrase, 'Meet the client where they are.' This means you need to adjust your communication, expectations and interventions according to the current developmental level that client has obtained thus far. You can not expect a 12 year old child who has been in survival mode their entire life to function at the same level as a 12 year old child who has had nothing but love, safety and stability. Trauma rewires the brain. PERIOD. You can't be angry at a child that doesn't learn or perform like the typical kid. It's futile and cruel. When people (of any age) get a diagnosis of any kind, adjustments must be made. We accept that when a car is in a serious accident it usually never handles the same way again. We are the same. In the simplest example - a marathoner will not run at the same pace or with the same enthusiasm when she has a cold or is recovering from a sprain. We don't expect her to. Always allow for adjustments in your expectations. We all need the breathing room.

Kids like Melissa who are abused in early childhood, moved or placed in multiple environments, have inconsistent or unreliable connections with early caregivers typically have a Disorganized Attachment style. Some signs of disorganized attachment in kids include unpredictable and inconsistent behavior, negative attention seeking, extreme fear of other people and avoiding interactions or extreme closeness and clinginess. Trauma stops healthy development and attachment in its tracks psychologically. When intense trauma occurs there's an arrest in development. For example, a person who experiences trauma at 12 years old may still react to situations like a 12 year old if that trauma is not treated. Ever see an adult throw a temper tantrum like a toddler? (The same happens with addiction too. When someone engages in sustained substance abuse, their brain stops developing. When they become sober, their mind still needs to grow from the age when addiction began.)

So, how do you parent a child with disorganized attachment due to early trauma? Sometimes it's the exact same way you would parent an infant. Be present, stay calm, own your reality, practice patience, and forgive quickly. Be mindful of your tone and facial expressions. Be curious, not judgmental. When a baby is cranky you don't punish the baby, you become a detective. You don't punish them, you take the time to look for the cause of their discomfort and try to soothe them. When kids have been traumatized, they need the same grace.

Kids who've been abused can operate in survival mode for years; well into adulthood. They pay attention to everything happening around them in order to assess their safety and figure out a game plan. All the things you try to supply them with (hugs, their own room, a quiet space, the ability to make choices) may be rejected or feared because these things are foreign and sometimes even scary to them. A kid who was harmed in the middle of the night may not want to have their own room. They may not want silence. A kid may run from being hugged because others may have violated their bodies. Having a full refrigerator with multiple options can be overwhelming to a kid who never had the ability to make their own decisions or deprived of consistent meals. This may not make sense to the adoptive or foster parent who didn't experience similar traumas. Don't take this personally and, by all means DON'T PUNISH WHAT YOU DON'T UNDERSTAND. Ask for help from a professional. Start small and simply. Give them what the world hasn't so far: safety, encouragement, validation, structure consistency and most of all patience. Teach them how to identify their emotions. Then teach them how to express themselves in healthy ways. Teach them how to self-soothe. If you don't know how, don't hesitate to get help from therapy professionals (mental health, physical and occupational), school psychologists (research if a 504 Plan or IEP (Individualized Education Program)) can help your child succeed at school and, if appropriate, seek medication interventions to manage symptoms.

Coming to terms with who your child is and isn't will bring up many emotions including sadness, fear, disappointment, shame and guilt. You'll fight with your child, partner and yourself to find your way through. Again, be patient. There is so much judgment in modern American parenting that you have to let yourself off the hook and give yourself permission to be human.

As you are navigating this space, set boundaries with yourself. You can only do so much on your own so take off your superhero cape. You will need to trust outside help. Like Diane said, you can't do everything because you won't know everything. And, set your pride aside and lose any embarrassment connected to your child's past and their diagnoses. They don't need your pity, they need your love, acceptance and guidance. Unless you hurt your child, you can't take their diagnosis personally. Do not create a codependent dynamic where you're absorbed into your child's mental health and you think that no one can help but you or no one cares for them except you. Being a martyr is about your past crap, not your child's issues. Work on yourself.

When you have a child who's struggling you can care but you can't carry them forever if you expect them to grow. Read that again. You can't heal them when they need to learn how to heal themselves. This is hard to do but necessary. They need to buy into their own health. You can't do it for them. You can't care more than they do. Your child has to take responsibility for their healing. Strict personal boundaries are necessary so you don't get sucked into their storms. Regardless of whether your child's issues were given to them biologically or they've acquired their issues willingly through addiction, you'll need to adjust your expectations of who you want them to be versus who they are at the current moment. This can be super frustrating to navigate when you're accustomed to a directive style of parenting which is needed when they're young so they don't run into traffic or only eat gummy bears. As they grow older you need to release the reins more and more and function more like a co-pilot. You'll learn that just because you tell them to take their meds, get 8 hours of sleep and eat a balanced meal doesn't mean they're going to see the value in any of it. Sometimes they have to have panic attacks before they realize they have safety plans and self care techniques that can mitigate their symptoms and relapses. When they fall DON'T add insult to injury with "I told you so." That's a great way for your child to see you keeping score and squashing any confidence they could build by falling and getting back up with your love and assistance. Be the soft landing for them. Teach them how to dust themselves off and keep trying again and again and, if necessary, again. Be their ally, not their judge.

It's important that you and your child understand that they have the power to make themselves feel better. They need to see the difference between using positive coping skills and doing nothing. Your child will make mistakes but do not punish them. Hold your boundaries help them connect the dots between feeling healthy and unhealthy. They need support in building the confidence to be proactive. Help them establish routines but emphasize their ability to initiate then maintain. You'll both need patience.

Self-care. I pound this drum a lot because it's so important. You can't take care of anyone if you aren't taking care of yourself. You need multiple pleasure outlets you're accessing daily so your stress doesn't take you down. You need to consistently and enthusiastically pursue self-care because that's exactly what you want your child to do so lead by example.

"Never give from the depths of your well,
but from your overflow"
- Rumi

Radical Acceptance

Radical Acceptance is a skill taught in Dialectical Behavioral Therapy. It's a concept that is extremely helpful but can be difficult to implement. The best way to describe radical acceptance is the phrase we've all become accustomed to... *It is what it is.* It's that simple. Accepting someone or something without tossing in potential or expectations. Radical Acceptance is owning the reality of a person or situation. Denial cannot exist in this space. You have to be honest with yourself about your situation in order to shift into problem-solving mode and make plans. Denial is limbo. Denial is emotional immaturity. There's no room for holding onto delusion if you want to achieve Radical Acceptance.

Managing our family and friends can be equal parts joy and aggravation. We have expectations on how our relationships should flow BUT that does not mean the other party has the same goals or intentions. Nagging, chastising, berating, shaming and manipulating does not move the needle in a desired direction if the person you're coaxing doesn't care about your plan. Radical acceptance is observing and acknowledging the obvious to reduce anxiety and frustration for yourself.

Here is what radical acceptance is not. Radical acceptance is not relying on someone's future potential and living in a present state of denial. It's not fingers crossed in the 'hope' something or someone will get to where you want them to be. It's awkward, anxiety-inducing and then, incredibly freeing when you've adapted to it because, when the same aggravating behavior arises you just shrug it off. The constant feelings of frustration and disappointment are gone.

What expectations have you placed on your child, yourself and/or anyone else in your life? Dig deep, own and acknowledge them. Did you want your kid to be LeBron James but he maxed out at 5'4" and can't dribble? Have you shamed your child for not being attractive, popular or creative? Have you forgiven yourself for your disappointment? Start by acknowledging what you wanted. It's okay but you need to own how you expected this relationship to look in order to move past it. Process with people you trust and who won't judge you. The only way to get past 'something' is to acknowledge then validate the 'something". Acknowledge all of your emotions. Allow yourself to feel everything in every way. Acknowledge the "ugly" parts of yourself too: the selfishness, narcissism, annoyance and frustration. It's okay to feel this way even with people you love. It's natural so embrace it or it will fester which can lead to resentment. Embrace it but don't stay in the negativity.

Karen & Trevor's Story

Rachel Emilia was born on September 17th at 4:15 am with a red face and flailing limbs. She was beautiful and I instantly bonded with her at the moment of her birth. Trevor Oliver emerged on a fall evening 16 years later after watching the movie "Chicago" and having an argument about how I hadn't been paying enough attention to the movie. Transitioning from her mom to his mom, I set aside my feelings to get the therapist and the evaluations and the social worker and all that was needed to make sure he knew I was paying attention. But, when I was alone, I grieved. I mourned the loss of my little girl who twirled with a hula hoop and made flower crowns. I cried as I put to death the dreams I'd had about being her mom and processed the fact that I was burying my daughter and welcoming my son.

My process of grieving was largely solitary. In order to support my child, I could not share it with him for fear of putting pressure on him. My friends and family struggled to understand the process I was experiencing. I worked through the shock of hearing my child say they are not the person that I had always experienced them to be. At times it felt like a punch to the gut that I absorbed and tried to heal later. There are times when I felt so numb and disconnected from the feelings of grief and loss. And times when the pain felt sharp as a knife slicing through the core of me. Moments where the pain was so intense that I couldn't catch my breath – I would look at Trevor and miss Rachel so desperately. I had to put to death the experiences I thought we would have – her wedding, her having children, bonding experiences as two women. And let go of all the experiences that we had as mother and daughter and rewrite them as mother and son.

There are still times when the grief catches me by surprise. When I see pictures of Trevor as a small child in that flower crown. Moments when I see my friend's children and struggle with the "why me" and the thoughts about how unfair it is. They are less and less as I embrace Trevor and acknowledge the amazing son that I have. Part of me will always miss Rachel. There is a piece of my heart that is reserved for her alone. And I choose to embrace the joy that my son brings at the same time. It is the marriage of the bitter and the sweet.

I spent years working in the emergency department at a hospital. I've had countless conversations with families during their children's most intense moments of crisis. Typically, when the family arrives, these young patients are experiencing their very first mental health issue. Unless parents have treated their own mental illness, this is their first foray into this world and for most, it's a scary and isolating world to navigate. The fear of what's happening can be a lonely place that harbors shame, anxiety, resentment and embarrassment. Unless there is a family history of physical, mental and developmental issues, most parents are caught off guard when it's discovered that their child has special needs. And they usually don't talk about it to outsiders unless they absolutely have to. There are support groups dedicated to the caregivers of children with mental illness. Seek them out in your area or create one. You do not need to reinvent the wheel or do this alone. Let your guard down and lean into your community. Finding information will help validate your experience and decrease anxiety. The more you know the stronger you'll feel.

Linda and her partner adopted siblings from foster care. The youngest has been a breeze to parent. It's played out exactly the way they hoped. The older child has been much more challenging. Linda called herself a "beast" and an "asshole" for being honest about how hard it's actually been. I asked Linda to share her story. She's an artist and chose to deliver her family's road to parenting in a poem.

Linda and Marcie

The Mourning After...

4 failed pregnancy attempts.

2 miscarriages.

Nearly 15K in IUI.

And with still no baby in sight, we decided to go another route.

We'll be foster moms, she said.

Just think of all the babies out there that nobody wants.

Their loss. Our gain.

Love is blind, I thought, and so off we went.

12 foster kids.

Six years.

And 320 days later—an opportunity to adopt.

Our dream come true.

And she looked just like you.

We waited for her.

Prayed for her.

Funny thing is, baby girl was never what we expected.

Definitely not what we'd envisioned.

No toddler talk.

No new baby smell.

She was prepubescent.

A whopping 9 going on 19.

But who are we to 2nd guess?

Because she was at least a start.

And so it seemed as soon as we signed on the adoption line

Away went Jekyll and out came Hyde

Lying, cheating, stealing—baby girl was a mess

Will I ever love my daughter

This has to be a test

Imagine us, best friends

Like those mothers and daughters on TV

That's how we hoped it would be

But as all her traumas rushed to the surface

I couldn't help but wonder, was any of it worth it

Decided to take a chance.

Bet on nurture over nature

That's when living with you, became straight up torture

Couldn't stand to look at you

Didn't want to be touched

Regret the day I met you

You've just hurt me so much

There's no love here

And it's killing me inside

My feelings — too hard to hide

Just looking at you makes me feel dead inside

So I try to fake it

Pray day after day that our family can make it

Fact of the matter is you may still be living

But I'm mourning all that I imagined

Because we're so far from that

I just wanna be able to like you

I swear to God I'd be happy with that.

What are your initial impressions of this situation? What do you think this parent is feeling? I sense she is exhausted, sad, regretful and still hopeful. How would you feel? Remember, curiosity not judgment. You can't hide these feelings because children can sense how we feel. It may be difficult for them to articulate what they're feeling but they know when something is off. Most kids who have experienced trauma have survived based on their ability to assess people and their surroundings for safety and adapt accordingly. They can't trust you if you're not honest with them or yourself. I'm not saying to blurt out everything on our mind all the time but, your feelings are your responsibility. Engage in talks or group therapy with others in the same situations. Cultivate non-judgmental relationships so you can share what you are experiencing. It's not the child's job to tiptoe around your inability to manage your emotions. They've had to do that their entire young lives. Don't create yet another environment where a kid can't be him or herself because they're confused or fearful due your behavior. Lead by example.

Many new parents desire to be perfect, start off with all those expectations then quickly burn out. You're setting yourself up for a fall because no human is perfect. I've found that parents with perfection complexes usually came from chaotic homes. They know their own childhood environments were toxic so they try to swing the pendulum in the opposite direction towards "perfection" which causes a different kind of toxicity. You can't be perfect in parenting so work on shedding that outlook. You're human. Own that you're not perfect and your kids don't need you to be. They need you to be kind, patient, forgiving and accepting. You're going to make mistakes, you're going to hurt your child by saying or doing the wrong thing, BUT, own it, apologize and work to recover from it. They need to learn they can go through the world not being "perfect". They need to know they can be forgiven for mistakes. They need to know they can take chances by trying things and when mistakes are made, you're there to catch them without criticism. Did your parents ever apologize to you for anything they've said or done wrong? If so, how powerful was that moment? If they never apologized, how painful was that experience? 'Oops' I really messed that up' is so powerful to hear. Saying, 'I was trying to help and it didn't work. I'm so sorry.' These moments help heal a child because you're apologizing for your own actions and validating their experience of the fallout. That rarely happens for kids but, when it does it strengthens bonds. That's the power of vulnerability. Your child doesn't need the "perfect" parent. They need a real one who loves them no matter what.

It's extremely necessary to understand that although your child may be 9, 14, 16 chronologically, due to trauma, psychologically they could be 3, 6 or 8 years old. Trauma literally changes the wiring in our brains. There can be arrested development which means your mind stops developing the moment a traumatic event occurs or when abuse is consistent. You'll be able to know how old someone is psychologically by observing how they react to stress. Have you ever seen a 50-year-old man have a complete meltdown and tantrum like a toddler when upset? That most likely means he experienced trauma during the toddler years that was never healed. Parenting children with special needs requires a special level of patience. You've been able to handle everything that has come your child's way until the moment you can't. It's quite humbling when you have to go outside yourself to get help. When it comes to your child, you are the expert yet, a behavioral specialist will have interventions that can help your child feel better faster. Don't beat yourself up, put your ego aside and get some help. Children from foster care have their worldview formed by chaos. They'll reject the calm at first because it's unfamiliar to them. They won't trust you or your calm for quite some time because it challenges their worldview.

Here are some tips that can be helpful parenting a child with special needs.

1. WITHOUT JUDGMENT be honest with yourself about your thoughts and how you feel.

2. Own the situation you're in. Be honest so you're not constantly frustrated by being in denial.

3. Grieve the expectations you had for your child's future. Then, look for positives.

4. Look at all the differences in your children and celebrate all of them.

5. All parents need a support system. Don't hide your situation from your village due to pride or embarrassment. Create a village if you don't have one.

6. DO NOT compare your children to other children or their siblings.

7. Do not ignore your child's plight but don't make it a crutch either. Some people use their kid's challenges in order to obtain and maintain victim status.

8. Do not assume your other children (Who may be low maintenance, quiet, get straight As) are okay being neglected, ignored or not the center of your attention. Do not neglect them in any way because they are "easier". This stance will bite you in the ass.

9. What have you gained and learned due to your child's situation?

10. Be patient with your children and yourself.

My conversations with children are obviously different. Many kids feel they are unable to be completely honest with their parents about anything. I've had adopted kids share how they felt they couldn't disagree with their parents or have any contrary opinions because they were overwhelmed with the message they had to be grateful all the time. That's the only emotion they felt they could express. I'm grateful I'm safe now but I can't say what's on my mind. Kids fear disappointing, angering, burdening or overwhelming their parents. I often tell children that their parents signed up for the job to love, support and guide their children no matter what so say what you need to say. It's sad when that proves to be untrue. Years ago, I listened to a radio interview of a teen girl and her father. The teen was evaluated at a hospital when she expressed suicidal thoughts. At the beginning of the school year during an assembly, her school counselor told the students if they had thoughts of hurting themselves they could come to her so, that's what the girl did. The interviewer asked the teen's father how he felt when he found out his daughter was taken to the hospital because she had a suicidal plan. He said he was "pissed off" because she knew she could talk to him but didn't. I could see why she didn't talk to him. I'd only been listening for a couple of minutes, and he had already proven how he was not a safe person to share tough topics with. His daughter knew he got "pissed off" when he didn't get his way. This wasn't the first time. I'm sure he'd shown himself to her many times before which is why she was more comfortable talking to school staff than her own father. It was him. He was mad that he wasn't number one on her call list when she wanted to die instead of feeling sad his little girl wanted to die. He made it all about him. This may sound nitpicky but, when you're working with kids and teens you can't dismiss or disrespect their perceptions. Their worlds are smaller, and they have fewer distractions than adults but that doesn't make their lives and challenges less significant.

So many of us have felt disappointment when revealing anything against the status quo to intolerant parents. Children think their parents are heroes that can do no wrong. As we grow, their capes come off and we have to respect that our parents are human. As we grow, we see that they can lie, cheat, curse, be afraid and do many other things that shift our perception of them. Yet, in spite of all of the 'humaning' children (of all ages) want to be in their parent's corner due to the child's forgiving heart. Don't abuse that love.

Regardless of whether your child is dealing with mental illness, identity or medical issues the goal should be the same - Love and accept your child while you love and accept yourself. Self-care and self-compassion are necessary. If you want your child to maintain a self-care routine, demonstrate that through your own behavior. Whatever you want your child to do, they must see you doing it with consistency and enthusiasm. If you want your child to decrease their technology use and read more books you can't demand that while holding onto your phone. If you want them to exercise, you should exercise and casually verbalize the benefits you're receiving. Don't be a hypocrite and ask someone to do what you're not willing to do because kids will call you out. It's not fair for you to expect them to be more mature than you are.

Working with Clients

Oftentimes the person who's acting out the loudest is considered the family problem. This person commands or demands all of the attention, much of the resources and patience and pisses off nearly everyone. In family therapy sessions, it's usually one of the kids that gets blamed as the root of all the family's problems. In therapist circles they're referred to as The Identified Patient. The Identified Patient is the child whose behavior is the signal of a family's dysfunction. Parents in denial can project all of the family's sickness onto one child (IP) and usually that child is the only one receiving treatment. If there's improvement, it usually won't last long because the child goes back into the home where nothing else has changed. If the parents refuse to look at themselves for creating the dysfunctional family dynamic, how can anything change? Over my career I've had dozens and dozens of parents try to initiate individual therapy for their tantruming, aggressive or sullen child when the child is merely acting out the sickness within the family. Every time I have to promptly say, 'You're doing family therapy or nothing at all." I have made exceptions to this when I meet both parents and assess their ability to change, or lack thereof. If I see the parents are the issue and they are unwilling to grow, I will work with the child on an individual basis teaching him or her coping skills in order to survive in their home. When they realize, "I'm not the crazy one" it helps validate their feelings about their situation which increases their self-esteem and confidence. Some parents reading this need to realize the distance your child has created between you and them is to protect them from you. This doesn't make them dysfunctional. It makes you dysfunctional if you either don't own their decision or automatically dismiss their decision because you're the parent, the older adult and you must be right all the time.

A client came to me to help process a series of destructive decisions made by her 16-year-old daughter. The teen failed multiple classes, was suspended from school for sexual activity on campus and she made abuse claims against her mother and stepfather which opened an investigation by Child Protective Services. The investigation was closed very quickly because there was no abuse. Needless to say, my client was crushed regardless. Her daughter had always tested boundaries, but her recent behavior took everything to a new level. The teen moved out of my client's house and split time between my client's toxic mother and her ex-husband.

My client spoke of an almost competitive dynamic between her and her mother. Her mother never validated my client's feelings by acknowledging her parenting deficits but rather deflected my client's sadness into an issue of badly parenting her daughter. And, it appeared that her mother and ex-husband were trying to alienate my client from her child. My client felt lost and unnecessary. The situation was flipped on its head because instead of her child being considered the Identified Patient, it was my adult client. Co-parenting was not working and without support from her ex-husband, my client had to figure out how to parent her child's life while being excluded from it. As my client begged for phone calls, replies to texts, family therapy, family dinners and quality time, she was blocked at every turn by permissive, dismissive and overindulgent relatives.

My client had full legal custody and financial responsibility for a ghost. She soon found out her daughter was skipping school and her grades were tanking but she had no way of supporting her. After 2 years of ups but mostly downs she decided to transfer guardianship to one of the child's grandparents. She'd fought so long and so hard to maintain her parenting role but eventually had to accept the reality that anything she learned of her child would come second-hand. Her daughter didn't want a relationship and her ex and own mother were working against her. It took a while to reframe the situation and understand that she didn't have to feel defeated. She could choose to set herself free.

"Parent the child you have, not the child you were or the child you want."
- Yeshiva Davis

Welcome To Holland
By Emily Perl Kingsley

I am often asked to describe the experience of raising a child with a disability - to try to help people who have not shared that unique experience to understand it, to imagine how it would feel. It's like this...... When you're going to have a baby, it's like planning a fabulous vacation trip - to Italy. You buy a bunch of guidebooks and make your wonderful plans. The Coliseum. Michelangelo. The gondolas in Venice. You may learn some handy phrases in Italian. It's all very exciting. After months of eager anticipation, the day finally arrives. You pack your bags and off you go. Several hours later, the plane lands. The stewardess comes in and says, "Welcome to Holland." "Holland?!?" you say. "What do you mean Holland?? I signed up for Italy! I'm supposed to be in Italy. All my life I've dreamed of going to Italy." But there's been a change in the flight plan. They've landed in Holland and there you must stay. The important thing is that they haven't taken you to a horrible, disgusting, filthy place, full of pestilence, famine and disease. It's just a different place. So you must go out and buy new guide books. And you must learn a whole new language. And you will meet a whole new group of people you would never have met. It's just a different place. It's slower-paced than Italy, less flashy than Italy. But after you've been there for a while and you catch your breath, you look around.... and you begin to notice that Holland has windmills....and Holland has tulips. Holland even has Rembrandts. But everyone you know is busy coming and going from Italy... and they're all bragging about what a wonderful time they had there. And for the rest of your life, you will say "Yes, that's where I was supposed to go. That's what I had planned." And the pain of that will never, ever, ever, ever go away... because the loss of that dream is a very very significant loss. But... if you spend your life mourning the fact that you didn't get to Italy, you may never be free to enjoy the very special, the very lovely things ... about Holland.

CHAPTER 7

Partners

In the early stages of connecting with potential romantic partners we usually put our best foot forward in order to present our best selves. Some call this perfect person our "representative". We are punctual, wear makeup and deodorant, hold doors open and probably have more or less sex than we really want to in order not to scare the other person away. There's no farting or littering and we all have a great relationship with our families. We are consistent and intentional in support, adoration and general awesomeness. But, with time, our representative disappears and our true self is revealed. Have you ever met someone great and then the person became even more awesome as time went by? It happens. But, let's be honest. It's usually the reverse - you meet someone and the more you know about him/her the more you dislike them, then a break up.

Outside of the narcissistic or user motivations, most relationships start with the best intentions. We want to love and be loved. We have high hopes for mutual growth and happiness. We want the best for ourselves and our partners. Some couples go the distance. Some don't. The reasons some relationships don't work are endless and it's rarely just one party that sends it circling the drain. Each party plays a part in the success or demise of a relationship.

Unfortunately, just like drugs we can become addicted to people. The beginning is perfect, but if the situation goes from a relationship to a relation-shit you spend the rest of your time together longing for the honeymoon stage, just like chasing a high. I don't use the term "high" lightly. Love can have the same effect on the brain as heroin. When we have sex, oxytocin, (the love chemical), gets activated and creates a bond with our sexual partner whether we like it or not, a one-night stand or not, you're bonded. If you don't want to bond to someone, don't voluntarily have sex with them. However, fear not, these bonds can be broken.

Yes, opposites attract and it can be a fun road but, sometimes those differences can annoy you to a point where you feel you need to make a decision. As model Heidi Klum says, 'Are you in or are you out?' No matter how footloose and fancy free you may be with a new partner, there are things you will need to let go of when committing to someone. If you don't accept that and surrender you'll drive yourself crazy and sound like a broken record complaining about the same things over and over again.

Theo's story

It's taken nearly 30 years to realize my wife has never been my partner. We get things done... separately. From taking care of the kids, taking care of the house - she knocks that stuff out of the park daily. When the kids have emotional moments and need tenderness - She's out. Maybe I'm an asshole but it didn't really hit me until I had a breakdown. When I'm in distress, I can't count on her. I realize now that I never could. With the kids I used to explain it away. "Mom's really tired, mom didn't know how important that activity was to you..." Whenever I'd have a depressive episode at least she kept the house going. Someone had to take care of everything: the bills, the kids, appointments, pets - I always left myself off that list but my last bout of depression had me suicidal. I was in a dark place, the darkest I've ever seen and I was there by myself.

Looking back I know I was embarrassed for falling apart and didn't want anyone to see I didn't have it all together. If I asked for help it would be proof I was a loser. Since I started therapy my self-esteem and confidence is better. I now know I deserve to express myself and get my needs met. I won't hide needing healthy things anymore. Reflecting back I feel like such a crappy dad. I was embarrassed for being human and passed that on to my kids. They're all adults now so we talk about it. There's so much that I need to undo, redo and dismantle so I can be a better father moving forward. My and my grandkids deserve that. But, I wonder if staying or leaving my wife will be better or worse for the family. My parents were complete assholes to each other. When you grow up with divorced parents you think life is perfect in houses where the parents are still married. Whoa is that wrong! I need to make sure my kids know that I see that now.

I jokingly started calling myself the Walking Wallet because nothing matters as long as the money keeps rolling in. My paycheck seems to be the only thing about me that garners any attention from my wife. That is my worth, my only value to her. I've brought it up, complained, yelled, threatened and nothing changes. Well, I guess something has changed, me. It never bothered me before, her ignoring me. I guess I didn't value myself or felt I didn't have a right to need anything from her. I realize I started feeling better about myself because what was normal is no longer tolerable. I've gotten to a place where I feel somewhat comfortable speaking up. I want to be seen but I don't know if she wants to or if she's capable. While doing some soul-searching I remembered that when I was a kid I tried to hide, blend into the wallpaper at my house. Life was safer that way. If no one heard or saw me I couldn't get hurt. It took me years to realize I was doing the same thing in my marriage. Maybe I intentionally married someone and created a family where I could be invisible and not get hurt. It's eery when you consider the things you did to survive as a kid and realize you're still doing them in your 60s.

Sometimes I hope that she'll read my mind but get mad when she doesn't. How could she? Shit, no one read my mind as a kid and that's when your parents are supposed to anticipate your needs. I guess I did that wrong too. I'm always told about the things I do wrong. Not everything can be wrong all the time but that's how I feel. Regardless, I guess I've decided to give up. I'm not asking anymore and I'm not going to play the game of 'content husband'. I'm moving into the guest room. Why fake this? The kids are old enough and smart enough to see this isn't working. I don't know if I'll move out or not. One step at a time. Even though I'm sad I am happy I am finally honest about how I feel and what I need, even if I'm with someone who can't and never could give it to me. I can't be mad at her anymore. Now it's time for me to give me what I need.

The assertive partner - aloof partner match is quite common. Unfortunately, each needs the other to keep the toxic cycle going. At first, it appears that the 'ball buster' assertive partner keeps the aloof partner in line and on track. The aloof partner likes to give the air of being confident and relaxed but secretly likes not having to be 'in charge' all the time. The aloof partner teaches the ball buster how to have fun, "chill" and be in the moment. What they don't realize is that the cat and mouse game of giving too much or not enough is unsatisfying in the long run to both partners because they're being passive aggressive. Resentments build quickly as the passive partner maintains passivity in order to control the dominant partner's moods. The dominant partner creates roadblocks and/or doesn't warn the passive partner about impending issues or potential crises so they stumble causing issues then the assertive (dominant) partner can swoop in and rescue the situation. Eventually a parent/child dynamic is formed with both feeling superior to the other. This is an ugly dynamic but not usually an obvious scene especially when played out in front of children. The lack of respect for each parent becomes a way of living for them and the kids absorb all of it.

When toxic dynamics play out in the home the children pick up on it and start acting out. The child's behavior makes it easy for the parents to ignore their own issues as a couple and instead choose to focus on the child who's rebelling, lying, angry or "being a little stinker". Outside perception is - If you put your focus on your kid that means you're a good parent. But, hunkering down and owning that you're in an unhappy relationship is a harder pill to swallow.

Tip: Take your blinders off. You're not Meryl Streep. If you're miserable there's a good chance you're not hiding it very well. Your misery is most likely spreading into all facets of your life. If you decide to try couples therapy, dive in sooner rather than later. Many therapists don't work with couples because the success rate is low. The success rate is low because most couples wait far too long to start therapy. By the time they start one or both partners have already checked out of the relationship. Don't assume your relationship will naturally improve with time. Doing nothing is a mistake. Also, assuming you have the tools to fix the issue can be foolish if you consider your tools were a part of creating the issue. If the relationship matters to you get help as soon as you can. And, keep in mind, couples therapy works best when each partner is also in individual therapy.

Tara's Story

I had just graduated from college in the summer of 2001. I was representing my sorority at our national gathering so I decided to visit with a sorority sister for a few days in order to carpool to the event. To occupy my time I jumped on Yahoo.com. At that time, chat rooms were a big thing. I saw a man whose chat room name made me think he was an Alpha. I had just become a Delta so I sent him a joke about being an Alpha. We chatted for a bit and he gave me his number. I shared with him that after leaving the Delta sorority meeting I planned to visit my family in NYC. He asked that I give him a call when I got up to the city so we could hang out.

I forgot to call him until I was packing to fly home. When I decided to call him we talked for hours Lionel Ritchie style - all night long. When I returned home I logged back into the chatroom and he immediately hit me up. After that we just kept messaging one another. Within a few months we decided to start a relationship. I can't remember who initiated this but I believe it was him. Within six months he sent for me and I visited him in NYC. I was in love with that man.

It was weird actually seeing him and spending face to face time with him on my first trip up. I remember my cousin joking with me saying he and I would just stare at one another in silence because there was nothing else we could possibly talk about. He worked in the finance world and at the time I was still trying to find a job. We talked throughout the day and at night...literally all the time. We got along well, and the conversation was so easy. He was very stable, grew up in a nuclear, very healthy, committed family. HIs family are leaders in his community including elders in his church, as he was. I had recently gotten saved so this was very attractive to me because at the time I had a deep passion and hunger for Christ and was a budding teacher in my own church. He would teach me things I didn't know. As someone who was raised in a dysfunctional family, I had voids in my life so I was excited to see his world because it was very different from my own He opened me up to another world (where people hung out on Martha's Vineyard and took day trips to light houses, went to plays and rented cabins for birthdays. He taught me how to dream big and "see in color". I'm not quite sure what his excitement was for me but I know he loved me deeply, I think because I simply made him happy.

In the church world we look for confirmation that we are supposed to be together as a married couple. Both of us received that prophetic confirmation on numerous occasions that what we are both thinking and feeling about one another was God. He introduced me to his family and his parents began doing marriage counseling for us - a red flag I didn't see until later. One thing I remember loving about him is that he was a strong leader. I can remember we would go on dates where we would dream about how our life would be after marriage. He would talk and say what he saw, I would write it down. It was beautiful to me. I bought into all the dreams he shared.

Going into this relationship, I was very broken but I didn't know it at the time. I was mentally and emotionally abusive to him. My words cut deep (and still do if I am not careful). My words have healing power but they also have very destructive properties. I would frequently break up with him when he upset me. I did not know how to have conflict and still be healthy. These were the red flags for him.

One day we are having a conversation about husband and wife roles. He stated he wanted to make all the major decisions in the home and I vehemently disagreed. I can't remember how this ended blowing up but it did to the point where I drafted a letter tearing him to shreds. I impulsively faxed the letter to his work. (In the 90s regular people didn't have cell phones yet and email access was still limited). As it came through, he was able to intercept the fax before anyone else could get it and he was upset with me, and rightfully so.

The next day at work I hear God say to me, 'The damage has been done, prepare for the end of your relationship." I got up and called to tell him what I heard God say. I asked if he was about to break up with me. He got quiet and I got upset. I remember saying something like, 'We've been in a relationship for about 2 years. You should know right away if you want to be with me.' He stated, 'Well, can you at least give me until tonight to make a decision?' That night he told me that since I wanted to know immediately he had decided to end our relationship. Mind you I was scheduled to relocate to NYC in the next few months so I could start grad school and we could get married. Regardless, he would not budge. He'd booked a flight to Carolina to help me move but he canceled it. Everything was canceled. Our relationship was over.

A family member of his lived in the same building where I lived with my family. One day I was going to the grocery store and we ran into one another. He was in town visiting family. After talking, we decided to restart our relationship and give it another chance and then, another chance. But every time we tried it I heard what God told me years before...the damage has been done. He couldn't move past how I had impulsively sent that fax. Each time we tried again we didn't last past a few months. I can remember telling him 'I know I'm a mess right now but I really believe my life will be different because I want to be different. I want to be healthy.' He told me that although he loved me, he wasn't in a place to walk with me on my journey to become better while not sacrificing himself in the process. It hurt but I understood him.

The last breakup hurt like hell. I spent years, maybe 10, trying to get over that relationship ending. In retrospect I realize it took so long because I had to untangle myself from all his dreams for us. I'd bought into them hook, line and sinker. I had to mourn the life I thought we could have had. Also, because there was the "God said that's your husband" component, I had to detach myself from the thought that somehow we would end up back together because it was God's plan for us. I believed this for years until he got married which was the year I moved back to Carolina. We had gotten back in contact with one another but he never told me. He later shared with me that he couldn't because he did not want to hurt my feelings. I found out about his marriage from my old pastor who mentioned it during a conversation. I was crushed. She didn't know I did not know. (About 3 years ago he found me online. He acknowledged that he should have married me, yada yada yada...)

I'm grateful he walked away because it forced me to really look at myself and actively choose to change. I realized that I was dysfunctional which I did not initially know. I honestly didn't realize that what I was doing was abusive. I had to learn how to be in a relationship with someone. I literally got a "practice husband" who was a good friend who helped me learn how to be healthy with a potential partner. I also had to learn I was still loveable. For a while I thought I was not worth love and that no one would love me because I was so messed up. In retrospect, I do believe he was correct. I don't think he had the grace to walk with me on my journey. It wasn't his job to do it. Where I am now has taken a lot of work and still does, honestly.

The flow of our adult relationships is a great barometer for how much you've healed your childhood trauma. It's naive to think your parents' love, devotion, screaming, fighting, ignoring, smothering, honoring and respecting won't have an influence on who and how you choose to love. Sometimes it's clinging to an unhealthy person, dismissing a healthy person, self-sabotaging or giving too many chances - What you have healed or ignored is on display in every choice we make. Be honest with yourself.

Candace's Story

To be clear, I'm not entirely sure that there was a lot of initial excitement toward Angela. We met through a dating app. I'd been on it for a while, maybe a year. And I had gone on many, many first dates. Some dates were ok to good, whereas some were utter disappointments and disasters. Frankly, I knew when I scheduled my first date with Angela that it would be the last first date I would go on for a while. I was utterly burned out trying to date. I think it was this feeling more than any other that wore down my defenses at the very beginning. She was pleasant to be with at first and she was reasonably attractive - two things that I cannot say about many of the people I had encountered while dating.

The more time we spent together, it seemed to me that she was a good person and that she had a decent work ethic. She was working with a prominent photographer and, she had her own apartment, and she was in a similar professional position to mine. Sure we were struggling, but we were smart and working to improve our situations.

However, there was a black cloud over everything that I seriously underestimated - she had recently sustained a neck and head injury while she was freelancing that was causing problems like headaches, fatigue, dizziness, etc. - basically, all the signs of Post Concussion Syndrome that I was utterly unaware of. She was seeing doctors and taking medicine and doing physical therapy to recover and, looking back, it seemed like every day/week she was telling me that she would get better soon, that it "only takes a few months" to recover, that she had ideas for what she could do professionally. On and on and on - FOR YEARS.

We tied our lives together fairly early because I had to move early in our relationship for work and her injury was causing her to miss so many days at work. She was going to lose her apartment because she couldn't afford the rent. So (like a fucking dumbass), I suggested that she move in with me when I had to move. Ultimately, I lost my job a few months after I moved and though I had some savings, I was going to have to make some tough decisions. I strongly considered moving back home to North Carolina to help out with my parents and to become a lawyer there. When I discussed this with her, she was not very supportive. North Carolina is not very accepting of gay couples and she didn't want to live like that. I didn't really want to move back to NC either - both because I don't like how homophobic the state is and because I went to a lot of trouble to leave NC years ago. I also didn't really want to break up with her. Still, NC was my first choice and my first plan. In hindsight, I genuinely wish I had done this instead of what we ended up doing.

Instead she wanted me to stay in California. However, to do that I'd have to open my own practice. I really only had one person in CA that I knew from law school that had opened his own private practice, and that was located in Palm Desert. So for months, I would commute to PD and stay with my friend from law school while he taught me how to find and acquire private clients. To afford to do all of this, and move to Palm Springs to really open my practice, she got money from her mother.

By the time we moved to PS, she had completely stopped working. She was still telling me daily that she would be better in a month or two and she had ideas for how to develop a private practice for herself while I built my law firm. But while she was saying these things, she was also drinking every day, she was heavily medicated, and she was going to bed around 4pm every day and not waking up until she'd slept for 14 hours. We had no sex life. I was really struggling to make ends meet and she was surprised by how quickly the money from her mother ran out. It's like she had no idea of how expensive it is to live in California. I was completely stressed out and worried about money on a daily basis.

This went on for at least 18 months. Amanda wasn't getting any better. She didn't contribute to the household in any significant way. I was responsible for our finances by myself and she didn't cook, so after getting back from work or court, I would have to make sure that food was cooked. She had a hard time driving herself, so I had to take her to doctor's appointments. She got overwhelmed when shopping because of her brain injury so guess who made all the grocery store runs.

By spring of 2017, I was so done. I was ready to end the relationship. I didn't care what happened next, I just couldn't do it anymore. Unfortunately, in April 2017, she had two episodes that led to ER visits. She had been diagnosed with a birth defect in her heart that she was supposed to monitor every couple of years with echocardiograms. Her last echo had shown that her condition was unchanged, but in the two years since that last echo, she now had a condition that required immediate heart surgery. Because of the emergency nature of her condition and because her only alternative would be to go back to Chicago for her mother to take care of her - and the potential for insurance issues to delay surgery and treatment - we stayed together through summer of 2017.

A few weeks after her surgery, I told her that I wanted her to go back to Chicago with her mom. I told her that I was done. Less than 6 hours later, she was back in the ICU with complications with her heart. Fucking hell! I was so fucking pissed off with her. I couldn't break up with her without it becoming life-threatening?? I felt so incredibly trapped. I was so stressed out and unhappy, I began therapy to work through my feelings of resentment and anger.

We ended up staying together for another year. I had gotten a job with a corporation in early 2018 and we had moved back to Orange County. We no longer slept in the same bed and hadn't since her surgery in the summer of 2017. We were roommates, but I was still taking care of her.

Ultimately, there are two things that forced me to end the relationship. The first happened around May 2018. I was cleaning my bathroom and we started talking about money. She said something about how we had to pay her mother back the money she loaned us when we moved to Palm Springs. She said that half of that money was owed to her mother by me. She flatly stated that I owed her mother $15,000. I told her that I had been taking care of her for 5 years with virtually no help and that was never going to happen and I left. When I came back, she didn't bring it up again.

The second thing that happened was that a friend from Palm Springs was going to come for a visit. As the date got closer, I was looking at the weather for the Coachella Valley for the days leading up to the time of her visit. I saw that the Saturday she was supposed to come was relatively cool, but the day before that would be absolutely scorching. So I texted my friend and told her that I bet she wished that she was coming one day early. She liked the idea of coming on Friday instead of Saturday. When I told Amanda that my friend wanted to come a day early, she went ballistic. This was actually relatively common for Amanda - she absolutely could not tolerate when plans changed. And I realized that I couldn't do this anymore. I told her that day that we are done.

We ended up going to see a therapist together so we could clarify some issues between us. I wanted a third party there to make sure that Amanda would really hear me. We ultimately did one session together and one session each separately. After that, she finally accepted that we were done. That I was done.

She ended up moving back in with her mother in Chicago. She left on August 12, 2018. To my knowledge, she's still living with her mother. I never gave her mother any money. And I've never been happier to leave a relationship. I wish I had ended things with her a year earlier. Every day free of that woman is a gift.

"If you're brave enough to say goodbye, life will reward you with a new hello." - Paul Coelho

So many emotions are stirred by our romantic partners. Enthusiasm, fear, optimism, sensuality, security. When things go wrong our inner child can freeze, run and hide or throw a tantrum. Do you want to find out how old you are emotionally? Get hurt and you'll see. How we handle our feelings in adulthood can reveal how old we were when we experienced our first deep hurt. Think about your last argument. How did you and your partner react or respond? There is a difference. Reacting is connected to our amygdala. It's the caveman part of our brain that has us act without taking the time to think. Thousands of years ago there was usually not enough time to think things through so your brain made decisions quickly because situations were usually life or death. Responding is the decision made with the mature mind. Reaction - punching a wall or a person when upset. Response - Walking away to think about a situation before making a decision on how to handle it. If a person reacts quickly they're usually coming from a highly emotional place - the inner child. A response comes from your higher adult self.

If you want to stop destructive patterns it's important to spend time processing after disagreements and breakups. Immediately queuing up the next partner right after a breakup or even before you've ended the current situationships is a recipe for disaster. Grow up or you'll pay your same dysfunction forward over and over again. I have a friend who is NEVER single. She's been floating from dude to dude since we were teenagers. She usually starts the next relationship before she has ended the current one. Years ago I stopped asking for her new boyfriends' names. I simply thought, "Same asshole, different name." They were all the same playing out the same basic bullshit because she never stopped to pay attention to her behavior. I stopped being available for her questions and stopped giving advice because the situation was never going to change. She didn't take the time to do the work to make sure she didn't make the same mistakes. Don't get me wrong, she wants something different but she's not willing to do the work to get something different. I can't want it for her. To stay friends, I had to learn to accept who she is and who she isn't. I set a boundary that I did not want to hear about her romantic relationships. We can talk about everything but her boyfriends.

If you want to grow you need to have the strength to be honest. You will grieve and it's going to hurt but we need to grieve our mistakes and our disappointments to evolve. Using the next person, food, drugs or any other self-soothing mechanism doesn't help you grow. When a relationship ends before achieving any goals you'd set (getting married, having children, buying a home, etc) it can be a major blow. So, feel it. Cry, scream, run, feel it. Ignoring your emotions won't make them go away. Please remember to celebrate the lessons learned, hobbies acquired, and amazing experiences and fun you had in the relationship. These are wins that you may not have had otherwise. It's sad when people think a breakup means their time was wasted. Celebrate your lessons. It's not a failure unless you choose to see it that way.

It's also important to accept our part of the health or dysfunction of our relationships. It takes two to tango and all of us enter relationships with our own shit. Our attachment wounds enable us to stay in toxic spaces for too long. If you notice you have the same fights over and over again, there's something you need to heal that predates your current situation. Take some time to figure it out and heal it. It's an amazing feeling to mourn and heal the old parts of ourselves that keep us stuck in the same old cycles.

"Let's be friends" How many times have you said that and didn't mean it? How many times have you heard it and rolled your eyes? Believe it or not it IS possible to be friendly with an ex. But only if you've processed the relationship to the point where you've made peace with being apart. No former couple can truly maintain a friendship if one or both still maintain romantic aspirations. If you want a friendship you have to be honest with yourself and ask, were you even friends?

If friendship with an ex-partner is your goal, honesty is extremely important. Are you still in love with your ex? Is he/she still in love with you? Are you hanging out due to guilt? Also, distance between the breakup and this new dynamic is necessary in order to shift mindsets and manage expectations. If you don't take the time to learn the lessons in your past relationships, figure out what worked and what didn't and, most importantly HEAL from the hurt, you will repeat unhealthy patterns. Each relationship should be an upgrade from the last one. If you notice you're always seeing the same crap, you haven't learned a damn thing. Stop and reflect.

When we enter relationships, it's important to be as authentic as possible, knowing we're always growing and evolving. Actually, we're not always growing and evolving. Growing is a choice not everyone makes. When growth is a conscious goal for yourself, it's disappointing to learn that goal isn't shared with someone you love. It's best not to assume you're on the same page about everything. I stopped giving couples therapy several years ago because I would usually see one person had moved on while the other was stuck in denial. The partner that has moved on sometimes looks callous to outsiders because it may appear they are cold. Maybe they aren't cold or dismissive. Maybe their mourning started years ago, long before any declarations of issues were made. Mourning looks differently with everyone and grace is necessary. I've found that something happens and a switch flips inside a person before the problems are verbalized. I changed my name on social media years before I separated. That was my first step out of the door even though I didn't realize it at the time.

As you're grieving there's a natural tendency to beat yourself up for "choosing wrong", "being stupid" or making a mistake. Don't do this to yourself. In those moments you just need to accept yourself for where you are right now, or where you were back then. We make the best decisions with the information we have at any given time. When we fall in love, we do it as the person we are at that time with the needs and communication skills built from birth until that moment. IF we grow (I say "if" because not everyone chooses to grow) we learn new ways of doing and being better. And, when we have new skills and more self-awareness, we make better decisions with everything happening in our lives. A coach doesn't keep running the same play when that play didn't work the first, second or third quarter. If the coach gets intel on their opponent such as: the quarterback was injured in pre-game practice or the running back is distracted due to issues off the field, he takes advantage of that information and runs different plays to take advantage of strengths and weaknesses. He doesn't stick with the old plan, he makes new decisions with the new information. If you're in a relationship, desperately want children and find out your partner lied about wanting them or changed their mind - make a new plan for yourself. If you bought a big house factoring in your partner's high salary then they got fired, would you stick with the current situation and drown financially or would you make adjustments considering the new information? You could decide to take in boarders, sell or rent out the house and move into something cheaper. Pivoting isn't just for your professional life.

Demetria's Story

He's always been judgmental but he really started getting angry, turning on people. One of the neighbors worked with him for over 20 years. He started noticing how John was showing up late and not really being motivated. He was always such a hard worker and seemed to love what he did. That all started about 10 years ago and has gotten progressively worse. He talks about suicide, "blowing his head" off. Unfortunately, that isn't new but it just sounds different. It always felt like crying wolf but it started to sound different.

When he got pneumonia it all went downhill. He got sick more often, forgetting things, complaining more about work. I knew that wasn't like him. I started really talking to the doctor. His driving was aggressive, speedy, not paying attention. His driver's license was taken away and that didn't sit well at all. I think I was in denial for a long time. Living in it it's sneaky, you write it off as just a bad day. Denial. I lived with this for so long. I'm realizing I never paid attention to how depressed he was before he got his diagnosis. Occasionally he'd mentioned his mother and how he barely knew her. I really couldn't understand how a son didn't know his mother. Now, I realize I'm a wife who never really knew her husband and what I know is changing drastically. The sundowners - WOW! It's miserable to see that switch flip from somewhat okay to irritated and violent. Alzheimer's is the worst! You're sleeping with a stranger.

I miss working together to make our property look good. I really miss the companionship of working together on the same goal. At the end of a workday we would plan the next day's duties. He would talk about the chores he wanted to complete - working on cars, chopping wood, building something. The next day I'd dive in to help and try to sort out a plan then he'd say I was lying. Like I'd lied and made up everything he said he wanted to do. I started feeling like a prisoner to his whims. I never knew what I was going to get.

When he was placed in hospice I didn't realize all the judgment I was going to get about making that decision. I started isolating myself because I didn't want to hear it. I didn't want anyone to be mad at me or think I was throwing him away. It's been hard. I don't like complaining but I should be able to talk about what's on my mind, how hard it's been to take care of him. How hard it is to know the perfect thing to do.

It's hard to hear about his episodes while he's been in hospice. He's been difficult to the workers. I know he's adjusting but I feel bad I couldn't take care of him anymore and now someone else has to. He bullies and yells at people who try to help him. He's accusing everyone of stealing from him. He's losing so much weight. He's bones, can't think and is unhappy. I don't know how long he has. If I'm visiting and he gets mad I've given myself permission to leave. I get in my car, take 3 deep breaths and drive home.

I try not to look at only the recent bad times and focus on the memories. Dating, getting married and buying our property was really a lot of fun.

Working With Clients

A client had strong opinions about a few friends whose wives had cheated on their husbands. When he found out his wife cheated on him, with multiple partners over several years, for a while he was so devastated he was suicidal. He felt his only options were dying or getting a divorce. He did neither. For years he lived his life in black and white but his new situation forced him to *see the gray* because he didn't want to die and he still loved his wife. He wasn't as black and white as he had assumed. He gave himself permission to change his mind. He did not have to do what he thought he would do. He wanted his marriage to work so he had to rebuild how he saw his wife, himself and commitment. Through this process, he was able to show the same patience he had for his wife to other people in his life.

Also, he needed to get mad in order to release his disappointment, humiliation and shock. And, he needed to cry - two things he was taught to never be or do. His "perfect childhood" included being put in a box that limited who he could be as a man. He was taught that having feelings meant being considered a 'weak' man. He felt he had to make jokes and laugh off everything in order to not appear upset about anything. Reflecting on his relationship, he admitted he'd seen signs of his wife's infidelity but didn't know what or how to say anything that could cause conflict and reveal feeling upset. He also needed to look deeper into his wife's upbringing, which he had never really thought of before. Upon reflection he realized she was emotionally distant with her family. He'd never witnessed hugs or "I love you" exchanged between her and her family members. She had a lack of healthy coping and communication skills and so did he because both avoided conflict. He also saw that their conversations were never about her or what she needed. She was always focused on serving other people. In a way they were the perfect matches for each other. Both were uncomfortable expressing themselves, both avoided conflict, both were differently publicly and privately in order to please other people.

He needed to step back and see all of her, not just the part that hurt him. He realized how much he appreciated her, how much love she showed their friends and family, and her creativity. He pushed himself to see past the bad and see her as a multifaceted human being. Shifting how he internalized her affairs helped his relationships with everyone around him. He won't say he's glad the affairs came to light, but he will say they've never been happier or more in love than they are now.

Mallory met Dan on a dating site, and they hit it off immediately. He seemed to always know the right things to say to make her feel comfortable. He was handsome, resourceful, and made her feel safe. They moved quickly, making huge decisions about their futures before really knowing each other as well as themselves. Mallory started noticing she could never do anything right in Dan's eyes. She started walking on eggshells as she did anything around the house. She wanted to please him and not make him angry after working long hours to take care of their household. It took her several months before she revealed any part of her romantic relationship to me. She wanted to focus on talking about school-related stress and was reluctant to discuss her family.

In time she felt comfortable, and we were able to explore all the paths that led to her domestic violence relationship. We needed to dive into her past because people will feel unnecessary guilt, shame and self-hatred for getting into these relationships without understanding the catalyst for engagement was created before the current toxic relationship began. We realized that each of her parents were emotionally stunted. Due to their deficits, they could not provide her with the steady emotional foundation she needed because they never experienced that either. (An important lesson here is people can't give you what they don't have so it's important not to shame them. But the flip side is, when you are honest with yourself about your foundation, seek help to fill in the gaps and learn healthy ways to heal and relate to yourself and others.) She did not have healthy parents to show her how to participate in healthy relationships so she dove into dating from a place of lack. This set her up as a magnet for narcissists and energy vampires. She began dating people who either love bombed her or drain u of her of all her kindness. She see-sawed back and forth between these toxic dynamics because of the path her parents laid for her. Her parents volleyed between bombarding her with their own emotional needs when she needed them - almost one-upping her when she asked for their help, they countered by discussing their problems which were always portrayed as more important than hers. Or they turned her into their peer by asking her for advice, money or spilling intimate secrets about the other parent. She was set up to be a people pleaser and dismiss her own needs. Once she realized this, she fought to establish her individuality and end the enmeshment with them. She needed to improve her self-esteem and create her personal identity.

After she ended her relationship and grew stronger, she realized how damaging the situation actually was for her. Years of childhood emotional neglect made her very dismissive of her needs and her ability to recognize red flags therefore susceptible to an energy vampire/sociopathic partner. When you've been starved of love and groomed to serve others you learn to accept people and situations that can harm you. History has taught you that no one cares about your needs or experiences, so you hold everything in. You become smaller. Mallory had been marinating in toxicity since childhood, so she had to wrestle with missing her abusive ex even though she knew he was not good for her. She missed him and hated herself for it. She also had to look at her parents' marriage, why they chose each other, who raised them and the reasons they were toxically drawn to each other. All of this influenced their parenting. In spite of her embarrassment, she discussed how much she missed her ex. The dysfunction was familiar to her because she was raised in toxicity. Having positive role models and healthy boundaries were foreign to her so she rejected that state. She decided to wait at least a year before engaging in another relationship. She didn't want to repeat the pattern.

It's important to grieve past relationships. It is especially important to grieve the toxic ones because there was a wounded version of yourself who was comfortable in dysfunction. As you learn and evolve, you will see how those relationships don't fit who you are anymore. You need to celebrate how much you've grown, and you also need to grieve who you used to be without shaming yourself. In the words of Maya Angelou, "When you know better, you do better." Don't judge why it took time to get here, just be grateful that you have.

Grief looks differently for everyone experiencing it so it's important not to judge. It's also necessary to know that sometimes you need to do physical, tangible things to help kickstart the process. I had a client decide to wear black for a while. It helped her reconcile the amount of anguish she felt by ending a toxic relationship. It gave her the space she needed to feel more emotion. Even if a relationship was unhealthy, you're allowed to feel sad that it's over. When people come together, each individual contributes to a new entity, the new relationship. The relationship grows, evolves, and sometimes ends. You need to honor all of these states, including the end, so you can learn necessary lessons and move on without repeating the same mistakes.

Wake up! Do you really think the people who hurt you understand how much they have hurt you? People will never understand the pain they have caused you the way you feel it. If your healing includes waiting on a big weepy apology, don't hold your breath. You also shouldn't assume you can't heal without the involvement of the person that hurt you. Whether they are alive, dead, across town or across the planet... You can heal yourself without the other parties involved. Imagine your highest, strongest, most confident self. What age are you? How do you carry yourself physically? Picture the Best You in charge of your life. Call on this person to be your guide in every area of your life. Have him/her take control. Meditate to call in your highest/future self to be in charge of you. Your future self has transcended the bullshit in the present. Your highest self is compassionate and kind. Relax into this loving and non-judgmental side of yourself.

CHAPTER 8

Friends

Our friendships are formed within the communities around us - our neighbors, classmates, teammates, coworkers. When we're young, these communities are chosen for us by our parents or grand-parents due to their housing decisions, usually based on financial abilities. So, we become friends with people who live like us and usually look like us. Most people never venture out of this comfort zone. Maybe you never left your hometown; most people don't. Or, maybe you took a chance and left and gained experiences that changed your perspective on previously held beliefs. We can outgrow some of our friendships because we change interests and grow in different directions. It doesn't have to signify anything negative about the relationship or people involved. It is what it is.

As adults, the saying, 'Friends are the family we choose' becomes especially salient when you have tenuous relationships with your core family members or differences in value with past friendships. When a friend reveals him or herself to be a trusted and reliable resource, bonds are formed.

Starting in my 20s and 30s, I realized I shared more intimate elements of my life with my friends, than I ever shared with romantic partners. Recently, there's been a movement stressing how our friends can be our soul mates, and I totally understand it. We all know the chances of romantic relationships ending are highly likely, but we don't start friendships with those intentions in mind. We all feel like our friendships will last forever, especially in the heights of our connectivity - high school, college, first jobs, stressful jobs, living in the same area. After my divorce in my late 40s, I had the realization that I shared more about my internal, emotional world with my friends than I shared with my husband. I've worked on that in recent relationships.

When we're young, most of our friendships begin with mutual involvement in fun activities. As we grow older, our friendships are created through mutual and sometimes stressful circumstances: marriage, parenting, work, health issues. Think of all the social media groups formed to help unite people experiencing the same medical or legal issues! Regardless of whether you meet at a frat party or a crappy job, allowing someone into your life is a vulnerable and intimate experience. All relationships require boundaries, if you want your needs met while feeling respected and so you're not swallowed up by another person's needs.

I've started relationships with people over mutual stances on social justice issues, politics but also ended some relationships over differences on the exact same issues. I believe the choice to maintain a friendship requires deep thought and consideration. Unlike blood relatives, sometimes it's easier to walk away from a chosen relationship with limited ties and compatibility. Since we are able to choose our friends, these ties can be even stronger than with blood relatives because our expectations of understanding our needs, likes/dislikes and boundaries are discussed more openly and honestly. We tend to be more vulnerable with close friends than with family.

Brian's Story

Shawn and I met in our 20's soon after coming out of the closet. We were at the same boring party, left at the same time and immediately became best friends. We had a lot in common, including being the only boys with a ton of sisters from middle class homes. We bonded over shared body dysmorphia. He was always down on himself and would joke about it. I could relate.

Shawn's mother died by suicide a few years before we met. The entire family was traumatized by it. Shawn went to therapy, but the rest of the family didn't. Sometimes he would wake up screaming "momma". He was so anxious he lost most of his hair and was really self-conscious about it.

I moved around a lot but we managed to stay in touch. He visited me in NY. When I moved to LA, I tried to get him to visit, but he was dating someone and wouldn't come. I don't even think it was love. It was more like infatuation or obsession, because his self-worth was always tied up in the person he was dating at the time. Over a couple of years he stopped answering my calls, and when he finally did, he said he didn't have my number even though it hadn't changed. When we finally met up we became friends again. Then, I realized he had no friends except the friends of his partners. If they happened to go through a rough patch, Shawn was excluded, exiled. Then, we would shop, hike and hang out.

Shawn had a bunch of different jobs with a good work history, but he didn't have a career path. He had jobs but didn't seem all that interested in developing specific work skills. When he was let go from a job and given a severance, he gave it all to his partner, John. He started looking for jobs, but got no bites. He said he wanted a job like mine, which was strange. I worked in television. My job and position were cultivated over 30 years. I'd been networking for decades and was working at one of the 3 big networks. I had huge responsibilities and was making great money and he thought he could just waltz into that. He just didn't get it. When he finally got a job with a real estate company, I think he got intimidated fast. After his first day he said, "It's a lot to learn. I'm in a fog." I encouraged him to try hard and ask for help, but they let him go after a few weeks. Then, he couldn't find another job.

One day when Shawn and I were shopping, we ran into someone I knew professionally. I pitched Shawn to her and she gave him a list of names and numbers of tons of people for him to contact. We got him a job at a loan collection company. On his first day, for whatever reason, he said he couldn't do it. His former co-workers were working there too. Maybe he was embarrassed? I tried to encourage him to ask for help, ask his trainers to repeat and clarify things. You know, explain it to me like a dummy. Whatever it took to get him feeling comfortable and stable again.

One day I got a call at my office from his boyfriend who asked if I'd seen Shawn. We found out that he hadn't shown up for work for days. His boyfriend said he's in bed at night and leaves every morning. 'I thought he was going to work'. I called him and he said, 'I just can't do any of it anymore. I want to be gone.' I asked if he was home and he was. I went to his house and he was on the kitchen floor crying. He said he was such a failure that he couldn't even commit suicide because he's such a failure. He told me he'd stopped taking his meds. I told him we should call 911. We were in the ER but they wouldn't let me see him. Later that day he said he was being moved to a psychiatric hospital. I asked how he was doing. He said he'd talked to his psychiatrist who can 'spring me out of here'. He didn't have insurance and was worried about the cost. I pleaded for him to stay for 3 days to get his meds regulated and get some rest but he wouldn't. I called the psychiatrist and bitched her out. She said he's there voluntarily which means he could leave voluntarily. So, when he called me I had to pick him up. She didn't want to prescribe him meds for fear he'd become addicted.

During that weekend his boyfriend said he couldn't take it anymore. He was exhausted after years of watching the breakdown. It's hard to help someone when they don't help themselves. He has 2 sisters, one married to a millionaire. His sisters were focused on getting back furniture from his ex-boyfriend, but neither wanted to really help by getting their hands dirty. He always had depression, was always sad, but this was beyond anything we'd seen before. They could see that he couldn't have a conversation. I offered him money and said he could stay with me until we figured things out.

I took him to the grocery store, but he couldn't make a decision. That's when my mourning process started. I realized I just lost one of my best friends, but he was still right in front of me. Many in my family take antidepressants, but I'd never seen anyone get to this point in their depression. The weird part is selfishly, my whole life just changed. Hiking, walking, laughing, fun - he was gone. Who's going to fill that void for me?

His sisters decided to pay all his bills, so he could look for a job without added stress. I kept thinking 'HOW'S HE GOING TO INTERVIEW!!! HE CAN'T EVEN TALK!' Regardless, Shawn applied for jobs. He had no money, had diabetes, but stopped taking meds. He saw a doctor who said his body is eating him from the inside out. I convinced him to get back on the diabetes meds and, within 3 days he was almost back to his old self. I was still mourning. Then, the pandemic set in.

When everything was locking down, I panicked about getting all of his meds. He didn't seem to be bothered at all. He'd leave the house, I'd call and ask where he was. He'd say he was walking around Target. I said 'You can't do this. We're in a pandemic!'. Then he'd come back home in a funk. He did it again and again. Once he called me saying he was at his ex-boyfriend's house talking. I told him he needed to spend the night there. I went to his sister, and said she had to step up and let him move in. I told him, "I love you, but I don't have the skills to counsel you and can't watch you in this behavior. He left and only answered my call once after that. He responded to a couple of texts with one word responses. He ended up in a separate bedroom in a different friend's house and got a job disinfecting offices in the evenings.

It was tough. There was no argument, no difference in philosophy. Our friendship changed because of mental illness. Up until I said it was time for him to go, I was the saint, a savior. His family texted and called constantly. After he moved - nothing. No 'thank yous'.

I don't have the greatest patience in the world. I have compassion, but it can't go on forever. I tell myself I did what I could do. I was there in the emergency room, helped him find a psychiatrist, and dealt with the endocrinologist because he couldn't think straight, because of mental illness AND diabetes. That's why jobs were so hard when he started. His mind was clouded and messed up because of the lack of insulin.

I've wondered if I was too hard on him. Could I have said anything, everything differently? Was I being selfish? Maybe I didn't want the hassle of being there for a friend that needed me. Unfortunately, I still struggle with that although he's not front and center in my mind. I try not to second guess myself because I believe I mourned him before he moved out. He's different.

It's clear that Brian felt sad, stressed out, guilty and alone. There were several moments when he was the only one carrying the weight of his friend's health. Frustration and resentment grow under these circumstances, especially if your efforts aren't validated or met. When trying to manage any guilt that arises when you're walking away from someone with big needs, make a list of everything you have done to help the situation and improve their well-being. Make a list of all the people your friend has access to, (whether they've burned bridges or not) that can help if they choose to. Also, validate all the emotions you feel (disrespect, anger, resentment, exhaustion) by listing the evidence that shows how you've supported your friend -whether they're doing it or not. (Some people don't take the time to carry the ball because they see you carrying it with relative ease!) Brian was carrying his friend more than his siblings were. Hell yeah, wouldn't you be angry too?

Respecting your own boundaries are important for many reasons. It's necessary to limit how much you give to others. Maybe you need to see how much effort one puts towards their own healing. Every therapist is taught this lesson, "Don't work harder than your client." The same applies to friends. Protect yourself because it helps keep gas in the tank for you to help others.

My Story

I met Thora through mutual friends who thought we would totally hit it off. They were right. We became friends so easily and so quickly that we didn't hang out with either of them that much after we met. And, to add convenience to awesomeness, we lived 2 blocks from each other. Party girl jackpot! Besides having jobs and friends in common, both of us were from small southern towns, had overbearing mothers and wimpy fathers, as well as the guts to believe in ourselves and seek our dreams in big cities.

Regularly, we brought each other to tears laughing about some seriously random shit. From dating, to food, to work, to men.

We never ran out of subjects to talk shit about. But, sex and men were our typical topics and there was always one man she talked about more than any other.

She met Kevin when they worked in the same department on the same project. He was in a long-term relationship with someone else, but that didn't stop Thora from falling in love. They didn't date at that time, but several months later she hired him to work for her on a project. They had an affair which prompted his breakup with that long-term girlfriend. When Tara finally had him to herself, she dropped all of her girl-friends. We literally never spoke to her again. I think her time with us was her way of coasting until she got him or any other man to occupy her time. I still miss her.

Jeremy's Story

We met through a mutual friend. We were inseparable, just like all 20 somethings with few responsibilities. Heath lived out of town and would fly in and out for fun. He was a super sweet guy, always laughing and sassy with a smile on his face. I never felt like he was my bestie, but we got closer and closer over the years.

In 2016 a group of our friends went on a cruise together. During one of our group conversations, Heath defended Trump and the situation got really heated. Defending Donald Trump is something I can't tolerate. I'm a gay man. I feel with him in power gay bashing will increase, raping women will increase and not just words, but his hate and exclusion will become leg-islation. Throughout the cruise, I remained friendly, laughed and joked. All looked fine. When we got back on the mainland, I was prepared to share a hotel like we did when we arrived in California. Instead of sharing a room again and flying back to the midwest together, Heath changed his flight without previously mentioning his intention. It was so rude and he left me with the hotel bill without conversation.

When I got back to Oklahoma I started thinking - my biggest issue is equality. Level playing field, no exceptions. I'm passionate about it. Why would I have this person in my life who isn't on the same page? So, I decided to pull back. I'm not going to call, go to dinner or hang out. He wrote me a Facebook message that read, 'I hope everything is good between us.' We went to dinner a few times, but didn't touch the subject of politics. A mutual friend said Heath was sad that I was mad. I said I'm not mad, but I won't spend time with people who don't feel the same about other human beings. I can't spend time with someone who bashes other beings.

Our mutual friend called me back months later saying Heath was angry (amongst other emotions). I said I didn't want a close relationship with him. "We're not of the same ilk." I completely pulled away at that point. After that, one of the friends on the cruise became one of my best friends. We traveled everywhere: Paris, Hawaii, Alaska, Mexico, etc. I found out she and Heath were chatting the whole time. Then she said they were going to DC together. I moved away in 2018 then got a call from a mutual friend who said Heath had a medical emergency while flying. Then I got another call later that Heath didn't make it. He died in his mid 40s of a heart attack. I thought WOW, no opportunity to heal or change the situation.

Ultimately, the rift was not about Heath and me - but society as a whole. He would do anything for me. But, I needed him to be there for the 18 yo. gay guy in Georgia. I weened myself away from him and started mourning because I thought there was so much we could have done together. We're adults, we're fine, but we need to be there for the younger people. I have a privileged lifestyle. It's roses compared to other people, so I donate and volunteer to bring people up and further equality.

One of the things he said before the cruise was, 'I can be a chameleon - I blend in. People don't have to know I'm gay. I can be around ridiculous people and they won't know who I am.' That's when I had to stop being silent. Heath had a 2nd grade teacher who he befriended in adulthood. He helped her run her farm. She had an opioid overdose and lost short-term memory. He brainstormed ways to help her. Before this he was down on anyone on welfare or addicted to substances. He bashed everyone. I hoped to stoke some empathy, so I asked him to think about their prospects, how hard it is to get out and escape poverty. You know, maybe drugs are an escape? They take a hit to forget. I tried to get him to understand they are people just like us but our opportunities were different. But, he was a typical GOPer - he didn't want anything to happen to personal friends, but bashed everyone else in the same circumstances. That hypocrisy really pissed me off. I realize that even if I can blend in, I don't want to spend time with people diametrically opposed to what I believe. That stuff hurts people.

In the 80's gay people were afraid to be seen on the news. There were unmarked bars and other safe places for us to just be. We learned that you had to hide to get along because if you live here you can't alienate everyone you work with, for or live next to. It was like compassion with a bullseye on it. There was a small circle for family, the next circle was for friends; the outer ring was for community. That's the south. If they know you personally, they may love you. If you have a flat, they'll help you fix it. When someone dies, they will bring food. My community will be friendly and help others, but won't help in terms of legislation and support. I've been mourning many of them my entire life.

When evaluating a relationship and deciding to continue or sever ties, in addition to mourning the fractured bond, it's important to also mourn the person you were when the connection was created. There was a time you may have felt happy, fulfilled, seen and accepted in the relationship. Maybe you didn't feel shame, ignored or disrespected because that is not who you were at that time. Maybe you felt that way but you didn't feel strong enough to speak up and set boundaries. You are no longer that person. You should celebrate your evolution while you mourn any fallout. The boundaries you set now show your growth up to this point. Applaud the stronger You, and what seeing yourself in this new light means for your future. Know that not everyone will want to see you shine, but that's their problem, not yours. We set boundaries in order to keep people in our lives. People who truly love you will want the best for you and will adjust to your boundaries. Severing ties with someone who constantly ignores your boundaries is self-preservation. Creating boundaries helps you thrive as the best version of yourself.

Work With Clients

Katie was 16 years old when we started working through her anxiety. She presented with FOMO (fear of missing out) in her school relationships because at times she felt her friends were mean and also felt like they didn't socialize without her doing all the leg work. She felt she had to initiate all their fun activities, meanwhile being the butt of their jokes and jabs.

For teens, their friends are the most important people in their lives. They are in constant contact and see each other nearly every day, due to school and social media. This level of attention and focus feels natural to them. When you are parenting a teen it is important to remember this dynamic without dismissing it. Parents often forget they acted in the exact same ways as their teens. When we grow up, and have more responsibilities, outlets and distractions it's easy to put the importance of these relationships into perspective. For our kids, it's not so easy, therefore be respectful.

Kate created boundaries and improved her self-esteem. Then, she was able to shift the pain of being rejected to empowerment because she chose not to pursue friendships with peers who don't value her. She strategically removed herself from the friend group so there wouldn't be catastrophic fallout, which can happen in teen relationships. She got busy focusing on herself after she realized she wasn't being served by her friends. Katie served herself by venturing into new cliques and activities.

"Stop feeling bad for people who had the chance to grow with you."
- Author unknown

To many, grieving the end of a platonic relationship is harder than grieving the end of a romantic relationship. The bond between friends is based on a choice, a decision. Ending a friendship can be devastating because the pain includes feeling disappointed when your friend's behavior opposes your way of being.

There are times when it's necessary to evaluate a friendship. We can outgrow our friendships the same way a couple can outgrow each other. When you realize your values no longer align, it may be time for a shift. In my 20s I had a roommate I'd known since we were teens. I knew they (gender disguised to protect privacy) partied in the past but it never directly affected me. Eventually, their drug usage went beyond recreational to what felt like a full time job. One night we were preparing to go out when they told me we were making a pit stop at a "friend's" house. It was a drug dealer's house. I was so pissed off that I ordered them to stop the car. I jumped out and walked home. They knew how my mother's drug use devastated my family but that didn't matter. It wasn't personal. They had an addiction.

I had to remove myself from the situation. I couldn't be held captive by someone else's addiction and risky behavior. I moved out. They didn't realize the danger they were involved in but I saw it. They had invited chaos into their life but I didn't. I pleaded with them to stop, do better, be better, but they didn't want that. They wanted a party lifestyle. I was different. I grew up in that crap. All I wanted was peace.

When you care more for someone than they seem to care for themselves, it is an eye-opening moment. When I was in college I had a friend who was an exotic dancer. I kept trying to convince her to take some classes, maybe get a degree and create a long-term plan in order for her to acquire skills to take care of herself and her child. She didn't. Instead, she decided to buy her boyfriend a sports car and pay for his education, before her own. When you're able to see someone's strengths and gifts more than they can, it can be heartbreaking. When you are able to see someone you love run towards destruction by making bad decision after bad decision - how long do you hold on? Sometimes you need to cut ties completely, or create boundaries to lessen your exposure to another's bad behavior. If you don't, this could lead to pitying the person or you are engaging in a codependent relationship; acting self-righteous around someone you love isn't fair to either of you.

A neighbor and her family were planning a move to the east coast to live near her family, which would help them save money. A mutual friend who had become very close to the family, even becoming godmother to the children, was devastated by the news. Just before their departure our neighbor said she hadn't heard from our mutual friend for several weeks. She said their last conversations were laced with curt, one word responses. I asked our friend what was going on. She said grieving the loss of our friends moving away was too overwhelming, and she felt the easiest way to handle it was to shut down and cut them off. She hoped this would lessen her pain, but unknowingly created even more pain and confusion, because the family felt rejected, dismissed and devalued.

Ghosting is "easy" (for people who don't have a conscience) but it leaves so many unanswered questions. Having a talk, no matter how awkward, is always better than ghosting. When someone disappears that leaves the other person with nothing to move forward with. Talk, cry, express yourself. You have the power to be the positive or negative part of someone else's growth.

Have awkward conversations in order to share your wants, needs, fears and boundaries, and hear the same from others. Here's another important aspect to realize about setting boundaries: Setting a boundary does not mean it will be respected and followed. People without boundaries or those with porous boundaries, don't really care about the rules of engagement set by others; they just want their needs met at all costs.

SO WHAT? Set them anyway! It will give both of you the road map of Dos and Don'ts in your interactions. Boundaries give people something to refer to when in doubt. If you express your boundaries and they are consistently dismissed, that could be the evidence you need to adjust your expectations of the relationship or sever ties completely.

While setting boundaries, remember that there's no need to negotiate with a manipulative or narcissistic person. There should be serious consideration in cutting these people off. Remind yourself of all the ways in which they have disrespected, harmed or used you. I would suggest making a list of these events to reflect on every time you consider allowing this person to take up space in your life. People need to earn your time and your heart. Learning to be content with being misunderstood or disliked is a lesson in maturity that needs to be learned. It's impossible to be everyone's friend. Let them be mad.

CHAPTER 9

Ourselves

"Nevermind searching for who you are. Search for the person you aspire to be." Robert Brault

Are you living the life you want? So many people live by default. They go through the motions making major decisions modeled after the people around them. They do what everyone else is doing without truly considering what would be best for them. Many bow to the pressure of their communities to engage in jobs, relationships or specific restrictive ways of living. Some don't bow. Some follow the crowd without thinking. Do you think your life should be dedicated to fulfilling the dreams of the family who came before you? Are you running the family business because it's your passion or your family's expectation? Every time I see a business sign that reads, "Smith & Sons" I wonder, are the sons really passionate about plumbing? My grandfather named his business "May & Sons" and he didn't even have sons! He had three children - all girls. His two grandsons were briefly roped into the 'family' business without a choice. Was your life plotted before you were born?

Do you really know who you are, or is your identity a reflection of the stronger personalities in your life? Did they create the life you're living? Does your life serve you or everyone? These are hard, but necessary questions to ask ourselves. Hopefully you ask these questions and many more before you marry or have children. Or, are you an addict? Are you using substances as a bandaid for the depression or anxiety for living a life you never wanted but felt forced to have? I know attorneys, engineers and doctors who are miserable in their careers because they felt pressured, by most likely well-meaning parents or teachers. When we're young, it's very difficult to stand up for what you want to do with your life if it goes against the plans of the adults around you.

Almost daily, I surprise myself with the things I think and do. As I reflect on the way I see myself now, juxtaposed to when I was growing up in a small bayou town in Texas, I'm astonished with how different I am. I'm proud that I've evolved by actively choosing to push past my comfort zones. I was intentional about leaving my hometown, living in other places and traveling to other countries where people speak, think and look differently than me. I've changed my career multiple times by diving into different industries and fields of study. I've changed how I eat, how I exercise, how I communicate and the way I date.

Growing up, I went to church weekly. Now, I do ayahausca, kambo treatments, forest bathing, and meditating. I've gone from cheerleader to yogini. I've gone from monogamy to polyamory and back, dating only men, dating only women, christian to buddist to hindu to a direct relationship with God, conservative to democrat to I don't know what now. I've gone from a shy, anxious and insecure girl to a confident, spontaneous and adventurous woman.

In my 30s, I realized that, at some point when I was younger, I must have made the choice to challenge everything about myself in order to live an exciting life. In my 40s "exciting" shifted to living a more authentic life. I've curated a life rather than living by default. I'm grateful my family never pressured me into doing what was 'expected', doing what's "right"' or living a predictable life. Doing what was done before, or living by others' rules, doesn't guarantee happiness, safety or success.

In this chapter, facets of personal identity will be explored. Living authentically is a newer conversation we are having. Identifying and living guided by your values is important if living authentically is your goal. This may not be salient if you were raised to follow the crowd or grew up in an enmeshed family where towing the family line was your only option.

If we're honest, most people do live by other people's standards and life goals. Here are a few examples:

All of your girlfriends are getting married, so you pressure your partner to propose.

Having children because that's 'just what you do next'.

Hating or floundering in high school, yet going to college without the desire or having a future career plan.

Do you know these people? They are never the first in their group to do anything. They don't do anything unique or ever go against the rules of their communities. They just wait to see what everyone else is doing: marrying, drugging, procreating... then just do that thing too. What if it were a foregone conclusion that you had to get married by the age of 22 and have 3 kids by age 30? Work at the local manufacturing plant, or are forced to become a cop, nurse, teacher, doctor or lawyer because they are the only "acceptable" career paths. You never live anywhere different, never explore other religions or food, and never date outside of your culture. Nils Leonard said, "Tradition is merely peer pressure from dead people" and I couldn't agree more. How about this: Stop being so damned passive! Who are you living for? You? Them? People are fickle. Choose yourself.

Real talk - Some people are afraid to be who they truly are, because they have to worry about their personal safety. If you have the opportunity and means to move to a safer and more accepting place, please do so. Figure out a way to be the real you.

But, if personal safety is not a concern... LIVE! EXPLORE! CHALLENGE! Life is too short AND too long not to live it your way. If the last few years have taught us anything, it's that life is unpredictable. At any moment, our behavior or the decisions and behaviors of others, can change our realities. These external situations can change us internally too. Think of all the changes you've seen in your circle: proposals, divorces, the great resignation, starting and closing businesses, having babies, moving away, death, etc.

Diving into or being thrown into 'The New', can be equally frightening and exhilarating, so check out how some very brave people navigated these changes, and came out on the other end stronger than ever. The following stories come from people who've made major changes in how they lived their lives. You'll learn about extreme weight loss, changing career paths, matching outer identity with inner truth, becoming sober, choosing to divorce and more.

Luke's Story

I stumbled through the impossibly heavy doors, through the foggy gates of abuse,

scraping dignity off my shoes, my exhausted heart torn to crimson ribbons, fell out of my wallet as I fumbled through it for my ID.

My bag was searched by thick necked guards.

My head was an aquarium full of algae and rubble. My legs were as uneasy as my stomach.

My spirit waited in the lobby, it sat there reading an old copy of Texas Monthly, an article entitled: A Missing Man, Race, and Old Familiar Wounds.

My possessions were deemed safe: Toothbrush, deodorant, socks, underwear, two t-shirts, one button down and a pair of Wrangler jeans.

I was asked to piss in a cup.

I did, Gamma ray liquid in a plastic highball. Just out of detox, I was clean for the first time in years.

I met a drug and alcohol counselor, he had a green dragon tattooed on his right arm, a gray beard down to his chest and thick glasses like tumblers full of truth.

He looked me in the eyes and said,

"You're in bad shape, I will help you get better."

"How?" I asked.

"I'm going to introduce you to someone you've never met."

His eyes were immovable, his voice was a white flame.

"God?" I asked, as defeat grabbed me by the lapels and slapped my face.

No." he said, "I'm going to introduce you to yourself."

I left his office and went to my assigned room. I vomited in the sink, looked in the mirror.

My reflection was foreign and I wept tears of rage and shame,

then tears of surrender and, at last, hope.

The counselor was right

I met myself a few weeks later. That was 7 years ago and we've been getting to know each other ever since.

The idea of recovery is a strange one. You must quit what you are doing in your life and start over completely. That was obviously easier said than done, but it is possible and can be achieved in many different ways.Twelve step programs are only one way to do it, and it is the path I chose. I am very grateful for the framework for living I found, and the lessons I learned there. This program helped me tremendously in myriad ways. Having said that, I realized that It was not enough. It feels like treachery to say that, but it is true. It teaches you how to stay sober. It does not teach you how to mourn your old self. I must say again, I am not here to denigrate the 12 step program. I still attend meetings regularly and have lifelong friends I met there. I am merely saying that I needed more when it came to healing.

My sobriety has led me to many alternative ways of thinking, and other kinds of healing modalities that would seem strange to the "normal" crowd. Normal is just a way of saying people who do not have a problem with drugs and alcohol. The normal crowd might have a problem with Zen or Transcendental meditation, strange esoteric traditions of thought and practice, Reiki, yoga, EMDR, cognitive behavior therapy, ancestral trauma work and shamanic plant medicine. Not just as a way of getting better, but as a way of life, a way of being.

All of these currents have led me to a very important discovery about my healing. I needed to mourn the loss of my former self, before I could move on with my life. This is something I never heard during my recovery. I had to take responsibility for my actions, forgive and "let things go." (A highly problematic phrase and a whole other topic.) What I never heard was that I must mourn my former self and my old way of being.

In hindsight, the emptiness I felt in early recovery, and even into the later years, has proven to be a lack of acknowledgement of the "death" of my former self. I discovered that this is the reason that one loses friends and the closeness of family members in early sobriety. In a sense, the person they used to know and party with and have fun with sometimes, is gone. For all intents and purposes they died and are buried without anyone in attendance at the funeral. This leaves the person in recovery bewildered and saddened. What many of us fail to realize is that the majority of the pain is because we did not mourn the death of our old selves. We moved on and didn't think of it as a death, simply as trying to get our lives together. This was a spiritual and emotional loss for me that came at the price of years of confusion and restlessness. I knew there was something missing, even after I had completed my 12 steps, but I could not figure out what it was.

When I finally came to the realization that I never mourned my old self, it was as though I could finally drop the weight I had been carrying around for years. A phantom albatross that I could never name. Armed with this knowledge, I not only felt the relief of years of pain being lifted, but that I had a new freedom that I had never sensed before. I can only describe it as healing on the soul level. Not only did all of my familial and friend relationships improve, but the understanding of my own ancestral trauma could be better understood and empathized.

Of all the years I have been clean and sober, the last two have been the most fruitful. I was able to see that there was a problem, identify it, and integrate it into my new, ever evolving way of being. One of the lines of my poem above reads, "We have been getting to know each other ever since." I was talking about myself. Now I can include the rest of humanity because I died and was reborn.

A big reason why so many struggle with sobriety is due to the shame they feel for past behavior - their own behavior or the ripple effect of the behavior of others. The past.

Getting sober is extremely difficult. Many studies have also shown that a healthy connection with others is the anchor that helps people maintain sobriety. Addiction and childhood development specialist, Dr. Gabor Mate' presents an astonishing array of scientific evidence showing conclusively that:

1. Addictive tendencies arise in the parts of our brains governing some of our most basic and life-sustaining needs and functions: incentive and motivation, physical and emotional pain relief, the regulation of stress, and the capacity to feel and receive love;

2. These brain circuits develop, or don't develop, largely under the influence of the nurturing environment in early life, and therefore, addiction represents a failure of these crucial systems to mature in the way nature intended; and The human brain continues to develop new circuitry throughout the lifespan, including well into adulthood, giving new hope for people mired in addictive patterns.

Many struggle with knowing who they are without their addiction. Perhaps the stress of not knowing your true identity outside of your trauma, keeps one in precarious situations, because the true self may be too stressful to identify or maintain.

Have you ever met someone who seems to always look for things to make them angry? Ever met someone who always casts themselves as a victim? They look for ways they may have been slighted? Those identities may have been implanted by your childhood trauma. With support you can change this if you want to. It'll be hard but it'll be worth it.

Jenny's Story

I almost never felt like I was a man. I always felt uncomfortable saying, "I am a man." Now, it's easier to say, 'I am a woman'. I just had to do it the hard way I guess. I never got to be socialized as a young woman. I had to walk the line of 'What's a woman supposed to be?' How do I know what a woman's supposed to be? How much of it can I do? What was surprising was how much I've always done as a woman and didn't realize. My transition makes sense because most people were never comfortable with me as a man. Apparently, I was sending a barrage of mixed messages and people didn't know how to react or respond to me.

As a man, I was trying to react to a script based on 1950's/turn of the century writing. There are things about being a man in that era I was never comfortable doing or being. Male aggression has always bothered me. That competitive idea that there can only be one winner, and 2nd place is the first loser, was always so bizarre to me. 'Hey, our team didn't win the Superbowl! I'm fucking pissed'. When my thought would be, hey, we got to the playoffs, that's amazing. Then, we got to the Superbowl. That's incredible!' The black and white thinking was always a problem. The American man is, in essence, boxed in a corner with very little range of emotion permitted.

I grew up with the expectation that men ask women out, initiate this and that. I always felt uncomfortable doing those things. The guys in high school treated their girlfriends terribly. What's weird is, I could see myself tolerating that but not doing it. Which is weird because I always thought, 'Why doesn't she slap him and walk off?' I spent a lot of my life trying to be consistent in things, but I was confused. I was of two minds about how people should get along. What I could see myself doing and not doing. But, the overlap didn't work.

Going through the transition process - at times I thought, 'I'm going into a new direction - the early payoff was when I made the decision to do it. Just like that, the rage just fell away from me. I'd experienced rage continuously from grade school through my early 50s. A lot of men experience rage, which is how they channel their frustration. Frustration is confusion, and men aren't allowed to be confused. Men are allowed to be angry. Anger is easier to understand and accept.

My counselors said that my rage falling away made a lot of sense. They also asked if there were times in my life when I experienced no rage. They wondered if I experienced it again, could I break the progression of rage when I sensed it. The problem is, while in rage, there's no time to stop and evaluate the rage because you're already in the rage. I was glad that part was over. My first experience with my serious transition was I didn't have to be what was causing the rage anymore. I didn't have to be a man. My dysthymia went away, because I didn't have to be what was causing my pain and rage.

My rage came from depression. My entire life, I was never able to relax. I didn't think rage was how a man had to act and be, but that's all I saw around me. How could I be comfortable with myself, or who I was in a relationship, when there's this deep dark secret? How healthy can a relationship be with this secret, 'I'm not really a guy.' The secret was crippling. I was constantly lonely and frustrated. I had severe depression because my life just wasn't working for me. The very things that are a part of a happy healthy life weren't there. At the same time, my counselors told me my long-term depression was a chemical imbalance, and had nothing to do with life situations. But, I had this thing going on in the background that was always there. It wasn't a short-term thing. Empowering myself to fix that, solved the rage and so much of the depression. Eventually I thought, so this is what it feels like to not be sad all the time.

This is what it's like to really be alive. I'd only had momentary glimpses of that throughout my life.

Still, I do mourn the person that's gone. I miss the person that could go out with the Marines and do the Marine thing - sneaking through the brush, riding in helicopters... I miss that. I struggle with presenting that without taking away from who I am now. It's easy to say that was a different life, a different you, which suggests I wouldn't enjoy it today. But, I'm almost 70, and that was a piece of me that I was successful at. I've had some scary nights but, for the most part the Marines knew what was going on with me. And, as long as I didn't bring it up, everything would be okay.

A few years into my transition, I came out to the Marines, but only when my retirement was secure. I needed to make sure they couldn't take that from me. When I came out to some of them, the response wasn't what I expected at all. They said, 'we knew and you're not the first to do it'. They were willing to accept it as long as I didn't break the rules which, at that time were, 'Don't make a pass at them.' The other rules, I didn't know, but I must have done them correctly. It's like walking a tightrope.

When I started In the marines, my job as a medic was to take care of anyone injured. I would stay in the middle of the group. As we trekked, I would blend into a third of the group to keep an eye on everybody. When they trained, I trained because I was a corpsman (sic). At the time I started thinking of transitioning, but they would have messed with my retirement. I was careful to never bring it up with anyone associated with the VA, the Active or Reserve military side. I knew I didn't have the resources to transition in a meaningful way if I had to leave. Maintaining my retirement benefits was a necessity for so many reasons, including my 3 children and wife. As long as I was doing my job they were okay with whatever was going on inside my head. They figured it out, which was odd because I was told they never had me in the section of their minds labeled as gay, which is good because they are never accepting of gay people. As fucked up as it may sound, I was cool with that, which came as a surprise to me. Self preservation.

I'd always been poor at taking advantage of my white male privilege. I don't think I lost that much, but I'm not sure. I'm still white, educated and physically imposing at over 6 feet. I've always worked in jobs that are close or favored towards women... except in Tennessee because... Tennessee. Now, I make 3 times as much as I did when I tried to be 'him'. I felt like I could finally acknowledge my feelings. It's okay to cry in public! As a woman I've seen the privilege guys get. As a guy I didn't feel like I had any. I watched it as an outsider and it pissed me off. The shitty things they do to women. I transitioned so late enough in life that I wasn't a prospect for young men. Which was a good thing. I'm big and I trained in the marine corp and in martial arts. At one point, I was qualified to enter an MMA ring. I can't be easily overpowered and no one would want to test that.

My upper body strength changed significantly after starting hormones. But, I don't miss the illusion that strength can solve a problem. My world never really relied on that. I met another trans woman whose strength was lost, and had to be mourned. Believe it or not, I had to mourn my depression. Depression had been a piece of my life for so long. Now, as I lived the true me, there was a hole depression had made and now there was nothing to fill it. I never expected I'd miss my depression, because I'd lived under that dark cloud of rain for so long. I often wondered, why do I miss it? With it gone - who am I? Eventually, I decided I don't need to fill the hole, because who I am without that will be someone I like more.

Transitioning is not just for people like me. I feel like all of us are always transitioning: Single to married. Child to adult. Unencumbered to parent or partner. Married to divorced or widow/widower. If we're lucky, we're always evolving from one phase to another.

Holding water was never an issue with a prostate. Immediate release is needed in minutes. Wearing a pad is part of my life now. Sexual intercourse is profoundly different than what it was, or what I thought it might be. I needed to know how to use my hands to masturbate. Or what it feels like to have someone inside of me is so completely different. I know the initial penetration is gonna hurt, working up to it means it could hurt less. It's brief. I never felt pain with a penis - never. This is REALLY REALLY DIFFERENT. When I got horny, it was easy to work it off with a penis. Done. Now, that's not my reality. The mechanism doesn't work that way. Also, how easy it was to mentally remap where the sensations are coming from. Same nerves but it didn't mean the same. Hormones. I heard taking progesterone was like smelling in technicolor. Smells mean more to me now than before. I could always smell my son. After hormones I could smell him three blocks away. I could tell by smell what my horses are up to. 5 horses - 4 mares. I could tell what part of their cycle they were in - whether they're in heat or receptive.

1. This wasn't nearly as hard or scary as I thought it would be. It had to do with other's response. How I went through this was connected to how people responded.

2. I realized men and women are more different than we could imagine and more alike than either one is comfortable with.

My mother took my transition a little hard, and then tried to pretend nothing had changed. My sister took it VERY hard! She blasted me for thinking I could ever understand what it was like to work as a woman, with conflicting demands, and never being the right sex for the job. I pointed out I worked as a nurse, and the first two nursing schools I applied to told me no man could do the work. That backed her off a bit. Two days later she called back and told me she had been talking to some gay friends of hers. She has been among my best supporters since. My brother asked me why I waited so long, and then went 6 years without talking to me. We are talking now. My wife had suffered a stroke before I came out, but insisted she had no clue I was struggling with this. My doctor claimed to be completely surprised and suggested I find another PCP [his staff might be uncomfortable with it.] When I told the people in town, about 1/3 had already figured it out, 1/3 thought I was gay, 1/3 simply said "that explains a lot." One of them desperately wanted to see me nude, I did not like him much beforehand, and that did not change my mind.

My children took it in stride. My oldest said it was weird and beyond what she could understand, but I had "earned" the right. I had and have some issues with that "earned the right" BS, but it's not worth the fight. My middle kid shrugged and said that it was up to me to do or not do as I chose. My youngest said I was still not the weirdest parent she knew. Later when I started trying to learn to play the bass and drive a motor scooter, she said I might be the coolest parent she knew of. My grandchildren are so young that the youngest does not remember me any other way. The older two remember me as both and for a time thought it was cool that I could change from one to the other. The few relationships I had survived transition, I had little to mourn in that.

What was hard, and is still hard, is the loss of the young woman I might have been. I am an old woman, but I have never been a young one. I have had to learn things in my 60's most women learn in their teens. I have had to learn without support. So, I did it mostly alone. Prom night, first date, flirting are things that I missed. And I missed it on both sides. I was trying to play my "part" with the wrong script.

I wanted to feel that moment when an egg is released. I wanted to feel myself be pregnant. Yes, I know and knew the magic of that is fleeting, and labor is no soft lit romantic joke. I still wanted it. I wanted to be a MOM and do the PTA thing, cook and take care of the house. I wanted to be a provocative hell raising young woman. I had no idea what that was, but I wanted it. Everywhere I could see examples and images of women and a life role that I wanted. I could also see a different life role I knew was expected for me that did not make much sense.

I am not non-binary. With all due respect, I think my life would have been so much easier if I were. I WANTED it! In almost any way you define "IT" would be close to or on the mark. It is not just that at that time there was no word for non-binary, I never saw myself in sexually ambiguous terms. I never had a non-sexual dream until my late 60's. I was horny a lot. I was jealous of people who spoke about losing their sex drive as they got older. As hormone therapy began to mute that for me, it was such a relief. If that is all I ever got from transition it would be worth it.

When my ex-wife suffered a stroke and became a stranger in my home, with whom I shared many memories, but little con-nection, I cried a lot for the loss of who she had been. Thirty five years is a long time for two people to be together. I have lost a few people to death and I miss them, but I do not often cry over them.

I cry the most for the young woman I lost to time without ever getting to know. I could not even comfort her. I could only hide her. I could rebuild the shell when life would shatter it. Often, I felt like I was looking at the world through the cracks in that shattered shell, afraid people out there would see me and hurt me. Some of my past I would do again in this new identity.

That other person is not dead or gone, but I was never allowed to live that life. I mourn the loss of that. It makes me cry a lot.

Anthony's Story

"Adversity not only builds character, it also reveals it," is a famous quote that I repeat to myself as an affirmation of the challenges I have overcome in my past because, in the blink of an eye, life can change.

I was born prematurely with a disability: Spina Bifida & Hydrocephalus. Getting the news was emotional and shocking. My parents had no idea that the journey they had embarked on would be a rocky road of medical adventures. They handled it with honor and pride. They say I was very active as an infant transitioning to a toddler. I was energetic and always finding ways to move, make noise and declare my presence to those around me. Taking my first steps was a tremendous achievement. Despite many surgeries and being drained mentally, physically, and emotionally, this achievement seemed impossible. The strides I had made seemed to baffle everyone, because the progress I had made to this point, happened earlier than anticipated. My parents treated me no differently because of my disability. I was fortunate to have many people in my support circle, and a best friend who still stands by me today, many years later. But, the halls at school seemed like I was running a marathon with no end in sight. I was stubbornly independent, wanting to do things my way. As a kid one of my anthems was the Frank Sinatra song, "I did it my way," thanks to my husband, and I was darn proud of it.

At the age of 8, I went camping. Camp Marydale was a camp not for people with disabilities, but included people with disabilities. This was a camp that gave me tools earlier than most. Resiliency, acceptance, and most of all, belonging. These tools would prove useful in building the foundation and mindset to thrive from the operating table at the age of 12. This is when my life came to a screeching halt, or so this is what I thought at the time. I was at a crossroads. The life I was living up until this point was about to change. I have had many surgeries. Some surgeries were to help me to walk better, others to improve my balance.

Nothing compared to being thrust into surgery in '92. It was something that would change my life in such a way that I would learn more about how to love life, express gratitude and appreciation, and thrive with a whole new set of adverse challenges. My condition had been declining, which is typical for youth at that age with a spinal cord injury, because the body itself changes. This surgery at the time as it was explained to my family was something of a make it or break it kind of deal. You would either come out with the ability to walk with less pain, or it could leave you using a wheelchair for the rest of your life. Either way, I was at peace with what my future was destined to be.

With the surgery completed and a long road to recovery ahead, my mindset never wavered from gratitude. I was and remain determined today, to live my best life, traversing my life using my vehicle of empowerment. The grind of 3 months in a physical rehabilitation unit allowed for education for myself, my family, and many friends, to learn about this new life I was leading. While my mobility changed, my heart and passion were on a path to carving a legacy. This is my life to govern, I am in charge of my autonomy and agency. Mentally, physically and emotionally it took a toll on me. But I made a promise to myself that post-surgery, regardless of the outcome, I would not change who I was or was destined to become.

Life was just beginning for me after the surgery as luck would have it. I loved watching sports and I learned about sled hockey (now referred to as para ice hockey) and challenger baseball. There were others in my community "like me" that had the same interests. The friendships I made were unforgettable and also a part of my life today. More skills for my toolbox – teamwork, competitiveness, agility, and cooperation were added.

As I continued physical rehabilitation, my toolbox would grow in abundance and would eventually lead to an overflow. Tools that most people acquire later in life were bestowed upon me at this early age. These were tools unique to me, and illuminated such powers that fate had prepared me for without me even knowing. Being groomed for a future beyond my expectations. Using a wheelchair, going forward was not something I expected, but I accepted. It has become my vehicle of empowerment. The emotions of using a wheelchair going forward, were never something that crossed my mind, because that was just the way it was going to be.

My family, in truth, was not prepared for life with me using a wheelchair. This was an education all around. Stairs in the front of the house needed to be turned into a ramp and my bedroom on the second floor was moved to the main floor. My father led the way, ensuring once I returned home, that our house was still a home for me.

Years later, I would continue to be authentically and genuinely me by surpassing milestones of graduating high school and college and being gainfully employed. A founder of my brand, Above & Beyond, an author, actor, speaker, and consultant. An Alumni of Distinction at my Alma Mater, a member of the Order of Hamilton for the city in which I call home today. There are more in which I could continue to self-indulge, but I am me because of those who are around me and I will forever be grateful. The man who I continue to be, is to support the next generation of people with disabilities, and those without disabilities, to bring together allyship. Where there is a win for access and inclusion that is heart-centered, there is a win for everyone.

I have to be honest, at no point were those 3 months easy. That time in my life taught me that if you persevere, the world becomes your oyster. The world is yours to conquer in your own time and in your way.

Tammi's Story

I met my husband when I was 19. He was 25 and had just become a lawyer. I was still a sophomore in college. He was smoking hot and very successful. I was eating Cup o' Noodles in my dorm room, while he was working with a decorator fancying up his waterfront condo in Miami, AND he was a great disco dancer. It was 1979. Was there anything more impressive than that CV?

We dated for a few years until I finished college. Then, I got an entry level job at a TV Station as an investigative news producer, reporting on the drug and murder stories you saw Thursday nights on "Miami Vice." They were really happening in South Florida. It was fun and dangerous, and my days were spent on fast boats chasing drug lords.

One day, I called in sick to work to go scuba diving, and apparently my bosses never got the message. I had been working with a government informant, a former homicide cop, who had squealed on his buddies. When I got back to my apartment, after playing hooky all day, the police had surrounded my building. When I asked what was up, and why I couldn't get in, they told me 'some producer from Channel 10 was missing', and they feared the worst. OOPS! It was quite an exciting life, and I wanted more.

So, I ran away to Club Med in Martinique for close to a year to teach topless aerobics. He waited for me. Then, I asked for just one more year to move to NY and try to break into TV there. He was disappointed, but agreed to wait for me. So when he finally asked me to meet him in Italy for a week, and told me he wanted me to move home so we could get married, I surrendered and went.

I built a great life with him. Sweet boating every weekend and we partied like it was 1984, cuz it was! We had two kids, I worked full-time, and my hubs became more and more disconnected. We split for a year and a half, tried hard to make it work, got back together for another seven years. My husband was not satisfied with his work life. He didn't like law and spent time investing. When one of his deals didn't end up as he had hoped, he went down into a dark hole. I had never seen him like that. He had always dreamed of being a judge but back then, you couldn't be on anti-depressants and get an appointed position like that. He refused meds and our life took a downward spiral. By this time my mom had stepped in to help when I was away. As for my girls, I was overcompensating for not being there, so life for them became a par-tay. Backyard BBQs every weekend, homegrown birthday and holiday parties at our house all the time and lots going on, always. When I wasn't working, I was creating magic for my girls and my nephews and my friends' kids. Life was fun, because I refused to let any sadness in. I just kept pushing it down and hoping it would go away. I really loved my husband and was devastated by our break up, but I couldn't help him. I had to leave him to save my own ass and my kids' too. In 2000, we split for good. It was on my 40th birthday, after two years of therapy, I finally asked him to move out. I even set up the apartment he didn't know he was moving into with pics of the kids on the refrigerator and all. I told the girls daddy was moving out, but we are getting a dog, and they were actually ok with all of it.

By then, I was working for NBC, and also had my own production company. I was traveling the globe on other people's dimes and trying to balance work and life as a single mom. My career was soaring! I won two Emmys, worked like a maniac, and ultimately landed at the Today show as one of Katie Couric's producers. Then, I began to travel even more. Life was hard, but there was never a dull moment. I also ran a grassroots nonprofit with my college professor mom. I was fried, but my daughters had a great life and we all came out okay.

I left my TV career at age 53 to create Campowerment: my dream of a summer camp for adults. An inspired and transformational place for grown ups to learn, connect and grow through the power of playtime. I had always loved summer camp as a kid, and as a producer, I had collected more than 100 brilliantly talented experts in dozens of fields, who had impressed and inspired me. So, I rounded them up, found a magnificent spot in Malibu overlooking the Pacific, and gave birth to this idea my mom and I had concocted in our heads.

And the crazy thing is...it worked! Oprah, Parade Magazine, the Hollywood Reporter and lots of other media outlets, wrote about us and Campowerment EXPLODED. I had never seen myself as an entrepreneur before, building something from scratch. I was a single lady in my 50s taking on the world. I gave 110 percent of myself, which meant boundaries just weren't part of my vernacular. I'm still trying to figure out boundaries. I'm a giver and a people pleaser. While we are re-igniting the lives of literally THOUSANDS of women, my spark was smoldering. I was tapped out, and my health began to suffer. After our Malibu camp was swallowed by the Woolsey Fire in November 2018, a few hours after we evacuated as we are setting up for 160 women to arrive, the stress ate up my stomach I ended up with a perforated colon, spending a month in the hospital before they removed 14 inches of my colon. Then, my mom died, and our community was devastated. I gave even more of myself to our people, who had learned so much from my mom Grandy, our sacred Campowerment village elder. I continued to ignore my own needs, until I was at my breaking point. I decided to take off 6 months and just travel and recover... and that's when COVID hit. By then, my 92 year old widowed dad needed me, so I moved back to Florida to help my sister care for him for a year. During that time, I decided to move my life out of California and back to the east coast. So now my boundaries are under construction as I attempt to take back my life at 62. Campowerment is soaring now digitally, as we deliver live, highly interactive workshops online, wrapped around fun and games...and now I'm putting ME at the top of my to-do list so, stay tuned.

Would I do anything differently? NOT ONE FUCKING THING.

Striking out on your own after marriage and career shifts will require intentional mourning. The loss of financial stability, companionship may call for a pivot in how you see yourself. Years of studies have shown how men thrive, and women flounder financially after a divorce. Alimony was created so neither partner is left destitute after dissolving a marriage, but what if there's no money to split? Lifestyle changes are HUGE post divorce, which can shake how you see yourself going from partnered to single. Raising children is even more challenging as one shifts from being partnered to being a single parent. The financial toll is especially daunting for women who already make less than men, but are saddled with most of the child rearing.

Stacy's Story

I grieve for the little version of me who was held to unrealistic expectations, which made me grow up way too fast. I don't grieve big moments or events, but small ones - like the ability to play and be silly with my friends. Playing is an appropriate thing for a child to do. That is one of the first ways to explore and create your personality. Unfortunately, I hyper controlled myself and never "let loose." I was worried about being seen as juvenile. How do you know who you are if you're masking the whole time?

I grieve for the little girl who was a natural cycle breaker. I had no encouragement or support because I was a girl who wanted to do boy things. I challenged so many traditions and could have been so great at things that went against the mold. How far could I have gone? What could I have achieved if my parents had been able to give me more meaningful attention and support? That is what I grieve, but then again, isn't grief just all the love we wish we could give, but can't? I try to see my grief as an inevitable side effect of truly loving all these versions of myself today.

Allie's Story

Oh, for the love of food!

Food is such an interesting thing to me. It is supposed to be used to fuel your body, and give you energy, but often it is used for comfort, celebrations or rewards. So, what is your relationship with food? Allow me to tell you about my relationship with food, and how it has negatively affected my life.

Since I can remember, I have had a deep abiding love for food. But, not the food I should love... I always loved sugar, snacks, fried food, pizza, etc. Believe it or not, I am an extremely picky eater. There are only a few amounts of fruit and vegetables that I like. It has always been a struggle for me. I always knew that I had a problem, but it wasn't until high school that I acknowledged it and started taking steps to change.

My typical day in high school would be breakfast at home. Sometimes I would have cereal, waffles, pop-tarts and anything along those lines. I then would stop at the coffee shop and get a frappe, that consisted of white chocolate and caramel, and would ask for it extra sweet. Around 10am I always craved Cup o' Noodles and would go to the vending machine at school to get one. Then lunch time would come around and I would go to a fast-food place or split some pizza with my friends. Throughout the day I would have a few Mountain Dews with snacks and candy in the afternoon. When I would go home for dinner, sometimes my family would make dinner but also sometimes, we would eat out or order takeout. Oh, and I also often had a snack when I got home. When I started working at a restaurant, I would order food from there. It was outrageously unhealthy, and I knew I needed to do something. Off and on, I would tell myself a plan to get healthy. No more coffee, no more soda, eggs for breakfast, chicken for lunch, no more Cup o' Noodles or snacks, etc. But, unfortunately, it wouldn't last long. It was difficult to maintain that in high school. I kind of just gave up, but watched to make sure I didn't continue to gain weight.

I graduated high school and went to college. I had BIG plans for my weight loss. I downloaded a Couch-to-5k app and ate in the cafeteria. I was very ready to be healthy... and then I wasn't. I got about 2 months in and everything went downhill. The cafeteria food was disgusting and I never wanted to eat there. Here we go again. It was always hard to make food in the dorms, so I started eating out and buying junk food that didn't need to be cooked, or only needed to be microwaved. I started getting very depressed. It was a small town with nothing to do. I decided it was time for me to move back home.

When I moved home, I got my own apartment. Again, I was so excited, and had a plan for my weight loss and to be healthy. At this point, I was about 225 pounds and I was devastated. I always told myself I would NEVER be heavier than 200 pounds. (In high school I usually weighed between 175-189). I joined a gym and I LOVED it. The workouts were fun, but so challenging, and it made me feel amazing. The nutritionist came up with a meal plan with foods I enjoyed eating. It was an amazing program, BUT over the course of 5 months I only lost 7 pounds! I was crushed. I felt like I had worked so hard and had nothing to show for it. Having very little progress over that much time was so discouraging. I couldn't afford to keep paying that much for something that didn't work. So, here we go again... I fell back into my old ways. I was constantly yoyo-ing trying this and that.

In 2017, I decided it was time for a change in my life... again. I knew I wasn't going anywhere in my hometown, and that is when I really started to create the Allie I am proud to be today. It only took 3 years! Lol! I will always be a work in progress as there is always room to grow in life. However, I can truly say I love myself. Now you are probably confused. How did I go from my eating habits to just randomly saying I love myself? Don't worry, I will explain.

Not only did I have an unhealthy relationship with food, I also did with men. Shocker. All I wanted was a man's attention. I put myself in dangerous situations and did things that are not like me. I reached a point where I did something I was not proud of. A relationship I hated myself for, and was ashamed of, but for some reason I couldn't stop.

I decided to see a counselor in 2018 to help me. My counselor had me start looking back at all the trauma I had been through in my life since I was a child. From my parents divorcing, being called fat and pregnant all my childhood, my mom trying to kill herself in front of my brother and I, my brother sexually abusing me, my dad verbally abusing me, my mom overdosing on drugs and passing away, and so much more. She explained to me (in many sessions and with a lot of work) how all that trauma led to my comfort eating and needing to be loved by men. It all correlated together and made sense to me. I never realized I was comfort-eating. I just thought I had a problem. Of course, working through that, at first, made me comfort-eat more but I still couldn't end that relationship. Working through all the past trauma was a very difficult thing to do, but it was very necessary. Finally talking about all those things was devastating to me. Throughout that time, I still yoyo dieted. I always did. I would get discouraged because I would be doing amazing, working out, eating healthy, working so hard but I would only lose 10-15 pounds, and then I would stop losing. I would become discouraged and frustrated and then fall off the wagon. This would last for a little bit and then I would feel so horrible about myself and become motivated to lose the weight again. I was working with doctors and we decided to get me on some medication that would help with my food cravings along with my mood. I was working with dieticians and Drs trying to come up with meal plans that would work with me and trying all different types of things. From 2017-2020 I was jumping from 250-260 pounds. I got down as low as 245, but was never able to get lower than that. January of 2020, I reached 265 pounds and I could not take it anymore. I knew if I continued down this road, I would be over 300 pounds by the time I am 25. I talked with my closest friends, some family, and my doctor and I decided that weight loss surgery was the best option for me. I knew I had already worked through everything that affected the emotional part of my eating habits, and my body just wouldn't let go of the weight. I also felt I needed help with the restriction.

I had gastric bypass surgery in October of 2020. I started the process in June 2020 with my highest weight being 264 pounds. It is now May 2021, and I am 149 pounds and I couldn't be happier or feel better about myself. I am eating foods I never would have eaten before, knowing that they are what my body needs. I am always mindful of how food makes my body feel, and most importantly, I am happy, I love myself both inside and out. I no longer reach out for attention. I met the love of my life. The saying, "you cannot find true love until you truly love yourself," really does mean something. I always thought that I loved myself, but I never really realized how much I did not, by what I was feeding my body, and the things I was putting myself through. I did not treat myself with kindness. Once I started doing that and truly loving myself, true love came into my life. I am now always trying my best to make sure that the things I do, are what's best for me. The people in my life are meaningful, I am true to myself, I am happy and most importantly, I love myself!

What if you no longer feel like the you you've always been? Do you feel like you're going through the motions in a life that once felt comfortable? Do you feel like you've been wearing a Soccer Mom costume? High-Powered exec costume? What's your costume? Costumes are always uncomfortable because they are a false identity, not our true selves. What do you need to do to take off your costume and live authentically? I'm not saying it's easy, but it is necessary in order to be truly happy. Besides, you're not fooling anyone. You exude your true feelings and desires whether you realize it or not. Others see you, even if you don't see yourself.

We get no guarantees in life. No guarantees of security, love or a long life. We are not guaranteed loving parents and a safe childhood. Despite the lack of guarantees, we still do however have expectations of how life is supposed to be. We learn these expectations from the communities we grow up in, movies and tv shows we watch, books we read or were read to us. I cannot say that striving to fulfill the traditional expectations of a happy life is a futile mission or necessary goal to feel successful. I can say that denying our authentic selves the chance to exist will lead to stress and sadness.

To be denied even the chance to speak openly about who we are and how we see ourselves compounds the frustration of not living as our true selves. Knowing there are some who would kill you simply for what you are is a frightening way to live. It means you live with a secret that your life actually depends on for survival. I have so many friends who left small towns around the world in order to live more authentically in large cities by blending into welcoming communities and creating families from friends they chose.

In the African American community "passing" as white (living as a white person due to lighter skin tone and naturally straight hair) was done by many, including my grandmother's sister before the civil rights movement improved our lives. In the 50's, one of my great aunts left Texas and lived safely on the west coast without the direct racism and discrimination she always experienced in the south due to her race. But, the fear of being "found out" added a different level of stress. After years in

California, she returned to the south and lived the rest of her life proudly and authentically as a black woman. White privilege is real. "Passing" as a different race can give the illusion of accessing that privilege but the cost is isolation from your family, distancing yourself from the richness and strength of your history and culture is actually living in a deficit.

My Story

I hate to admit how much I love distraction: food, travel, work, sex, cooking. I often pride myself on being a distraction for other people. I love giving my all to something that's totally unnecessary which temporarily spares me from whatever misperceived pain I could potentially experience. It's complicated, it's juvenile, it's simple self-sabotage. Only after I moved from Washington and back to Texas did I realize how much I delayed grieving my marriage. Three days before a trip to Costa Rica I cried from the moment I woke up until I fell asleep that night. During that day I also realized that the following day was the 7th anniversary of my mother's death. That didn't hit me that hard because we were never close. What did hit me was realizing how strong my pain was about my divorce that was finalized almost 3 years prior... even if I initiated it. This person was a positive force in my life in many ways. He let me be a damsel in distress because I needed to heal the lack of stability and support I needed in childhood. With him I healed many parts of myself, and ironically, grew myself right out of the relationship.

Even though I only wanted to be a mother for a brief time, I'm still mourning the mother I didn't become and the marriage I walked away from. I've just stopped crying over it. We've both moved on, and are experiencing the lives we wanted all along, just not with each other. I'm actively trying to mourn the scared girl and woman I have been. Only within this decade, have I learned that I've been living in survival mode my entire life - DECADES after living an existence that needed to be survived. I hate to admit I wanted to be rescued, because even in my 40s, I still needed to be rescued. Fierce independence is the result of childhood trauma. When you don't have access to security you spend the rest of your life seeking it whether you want to admit it or not. I didn't want to depend on anyone.

The lasting effects of childhood abuse have wreaked havoc on so many of my adult pursuits. This book has been stopped and started multiple times in recent years, because sitting still to focus is a challenge. I've been too hard on myself for too long. During a session, a client declared that she had ADHD. I was shocked. I asked what she was experiencing, in order to come to that conclusion. To my surprise, I realized I had every single symptom she described - not paying attention to details and making careless mistakes with paperwork, being easily distracted, verbal impulsivity, failing to meet deadlines and avoiding tasks that require concentration. (Did I mention how many books I started before this one and how long it's taken me to write this one???) My client was accepting this part of her brain, and seemed okay with it, so I decided I was going to be okay with it too.

I came across an article about self-control issues, which introduced a concept to me called, "Insufficient Self-Control Scheme." It describes the difficulty in moderating impulses. I'm trying to mourn the fears that have stopped me from completing amazing projects over the years. I know my history of starting and stopping things, wanting things to be perfect and fear of sharing my creativity, are all trauma responses. I'm excited to know the me that isn't ruled by fear. The fear of messing up, the fear of disappointing others before disappointing myself has stopped. Fear is too strong. I am actively creating a new identity devoid of it.

These epiphanies, these realizations help me understand that I'm done with the life I thought I wanted. I release myself from the person I tried to be. I release myself from the person I hoped I could be. I release others for not being what I thought I wanted them to be for me.

Boundaries are extremely important in all relationships, most importantly, the relationship with ourselves. When starting new love relationships, it can be hard to establish them, because we don't want to look unappealing. We don't want to appear as uptight, needy, controlling, or even liking the other person more than they may like us. We're afraid of scaring someone off with our wants and needs. Starting a new relationship can feel like you're walking a tightrope, but we shouldn't hold back. Say what you need to say, ask for the things you want. If not, your 'representative' (the fake/perfect you) will absolutely send the wrong signals, and misunderstandings will occur. You can't have someone falling in love with the fake you. When the real you comes out, usually during a stressful moment, the other person will feel betrayed and rightfully so. Make sure you're giving yourself the same consideration that you would give to someone else you're trying to impress. The most important audience should be yourself. Impress yourself with your authenticity.

Do a self-assessment of your behavior in past relationships. Analyze what worked and what didn't. Have you gotten the same complaints from multiple past partners? Do you know what your triggers are? If not, you need to know. It's important to know what makes you happy, what calms you down, what scares you and what stresses you. It's important for you to acknowledge your triggers, and be honest with yourself. It can be helpful to express your triggers to others, but it's not their job to tiptoe around your triggers. It's your job to work through your triggers, so they are no longer remain triggers. Getting to know someone new, requires you to dive in with reckless abandon, while setting boundaries with yourself first. Figure out who you are with reckless abandon.

It's important to forgive yourself for all of the things you do to protect yourself. If those things harm other people, you need to incorporate new coping strategies in your life. Being traumatized is not an excuse for bad behavior. You're not a bad person for all the ways you have tried to manage your pain. Keep in mind that you also bear the responsibility for not sharing your pain with others when you don't grow.

A significant part of our healing comes in the form of mourning. It's important to address the support you didn't get, but should have gotten, from your family and friends during difficult transitions. The fear of being exiled and ignored by the people we love is what keeps us in hiding. The ability to flourish in life improves when we have supportive people in our lives. If those people have loudly expressed their dislike for who you are, who you love or how you want to live it is heartbreaking. Thoughts and emotions that are common in these scenarios include disappointment, fear, feeling inadequate, overwhelm, shock, anger, fragility and loneliness.

Change, even when we initiate the change, can bring on a sense of loss. Grief is our response to that loss. Grief can be tears, but it can also present in a myriad of ways including appetite and weight fluctuations, risky behavior like self-harm, substance abuse, excessive shopping and promiscuity. Grief can also be in the form of self-isolation, altered outward appearances like new hairstyles, body piercings, and new tattoos. Feeling helpless or out of control due to new circumstances can have us looking for something we can control to soothe us. The key is finding positive and healthy ways to soothe that don't cause other problems.

A practical therapeutic intervention I like is called Opposite Action. It's a skill within Dialectical Behavioral Therapy. It's simple in that you just choose to do the exact opposite, of whatever your normal reaction would be to a situation. For example, how do you typically handle a romantic breakup? Do you isolate yourself? Let's say you stay home, eat lots of carbs and drink alcohol excessively. Opposite Action would be choosing to do the exact opposite of one, or all of those things. Instead of shutting down and being alone, you could choose instead to go on walks with girlfriends. You could set consistent dates to spend time with friends and/or join a gym. Instead of emotionally eating and numbing by drinking you could adopt a new health routine that incorporated healthy eating and clean hydration. If you feel rejected, instead of grabbing a cocktail and numbing yourself... You could open up and talk about what you're feeling. Process the feelings in order to let them go instead of burying them, not learning from them and repeating the pattern again with the next breakup. Feelings are temporary and thoughts are fleeting. Don't let them scare you. Doing the exact opposite of what you would normally do, can give you a better perspective on your current situation. It can also lay the groundwork for new insights and lessons you can take into your next relationships.

If you want to change how you respond to a situation you experience regularly, try starting with changing one of your behaviors. This exercise requires honesty. First, write down how you react to a common situation: include your thoughts and your feelings about it, along with your behavioral response to the situation. Secondly, look at all of your actions/behaviors. Then, choose to do the complete opposite of that behavior. You will most likely feel better, which will change your thoughts about the situation. This is an exercise in Cognitive Behavioral Therapy, specifically called the CBT Triangle, which shows the connections between our thoughts, feelings and actions.

Working With Clients

When children live in chaotic homes, school becomes a part of their system, it can definitely be a safe place. A few years ago a teacher reached out urging me to work with one of her students. Sam was a 16 year old transgender male. This work can be challenging to navigate and even harder when you live in a small town with no mentors.

Sam grew up in a household with a recovering drug addict mother, whose latest addiction was religion, which happens quite often in recovery circles. I believe religions are supposed to be inclusive, supportive and lack judgment. Unfortunately, that's not always the case. Some people can use their religion to control or bully others to meet narrow criteria for inclusion in the family unit. Sam's mother had this approach.

Sam's father was a little more accepting, but not by much. He refused to use his child's preferred pronouns and threatened to kick him out often. Can you imagine how hard it is to fight for your identity with the people that created it? Sam was in a difficult position of wanting to love, honor and respect his parents, yet hated them for not loving, honoring or respecting his identity. Can you imagine trying to navigate this as a teen?

Sam's mother angrily mourned him for not being the frilly daughter she wanted. The problem is, the way she mourned, pushed her and her son apart. One of the first attachment ruptures was Sam's mother's drug abuse throughout his childhood. Although his mother was physically present, she wasn't there emotionally to nurture her children. Sam and his brother were emotionally neglected. The family never fully recovered from mom's emotional distance.

As a child Sam thought he was a lesbian. For a while that brought him relief. Lesbians were at least somewhat common. Even then he didn't dress "girlie". He was always casual and boyish. Regardless of what he wore or did, his parents never approved and they openly favored his younger brother for being "a real man." His younger brother wasn't a safe space either. He liked that he was favored by their parents over Sam.

Sam felt alone, but wanted to feel comfortable in his skin under that roof. He silently struggled with body dysmorphia, suicidal thoughts, self-harm and anxiety. He had to mourn his former self as well as mourn who his parents were supposed to be for him as their child. He felt like he disappointed his parents, and grieved how they disappointed him. He had strong feelings of guilt, loss and loneliness, that kept his suicidal ideation as a constant companion. Suicide was a way out for Sam, but not a relief, because his mother's religious views shamed that as well.

Part of Sam's treatment included weekly talk therapy and antidepressants. He also had to create a self-care routine, unlike his family's usual method of self-medicating with drugs, alcohol and religion. Sam stopped smoking marijuana and started tuning his family out. He engaged in hobbies that got him out of the house and also found a job. Although he felt sadness for not being accepted by his parents, he worked hard to create his own identity and support system outside of his family. This increased his self-esteem. While spending time in LGBTQ+ communities, he found friends and mentors who became the family he needed.

In the beginning of our therapeutic relationship I told Sam many times that gender transition was not an expertise of mine. I was afraid to harm him if I was learning about trans issues while simultaneously counseling him. I didn't think that was fair to him. When I mentioned potentially transferring him to a more skilled therapist in this realm, he was upset and felt rejected, which I didn't anticipate. He said he didn't want to transfer to a new therapist. He said he was comfortable with me, since we had an established relationship that trumped having all the answers at my fingertips. He also said the consistency in our weekly sessions grounded him. We worked on personal boundaries, in order to protect him from his parents' unrealistic expectations. We also completed a genogram, so Sam could see his family's history of ostracizing members who didn't fall in line with their enmeshed patterns. This helped Sam put into perspective his family's need for an enemy in each generation, an 'other' to marginalize, while toxic or abusive behavior ran rampant. Ultimately, Sam was able to differentiate himself from his enmeshed family.

PART III

CHAPTER 10

Forgiveness

> *"Forgiving you is my gift to you.*
> *Moving on is my gift to myself."*
> *- Buddist Proverb*

Before I talk about what forgiveness is, let's discuss what it isn't. Forgiveness is not giving permission to people to harm you with their behavior and viewpoints. Forgiveness is not completely ignoring how someone's words and actions affect you. Forgiving is not forgetting. Forgiveness is not saying the words yet continuing to hold the issue over the offender's head by mentioning it repeatedly.

Forgiveness is a choice to work through an incident that brought harm to you by someone else. Forgiveness is intentionally letting go. The act of forgiving is a personal one and can look different to everyone. Forgiveness can look however you need it to look, for you to maintain a relationship you hold dear. For forgiveness to stick, you must maintain some level of respect for yourself. You can forgive someone without ever having a conversation with them. You can forgive someone who is dead. I had someone tell me they dreamed of a conversation with a destructive former friend, and felt she forgave her estranged girlfriend while dreaming. She woke up renewed. The power of forgiveness lies in our own hearts, minds, and our hands, and can be very powerful. Forgiveness frees the forgiver. It allows you to let go of tough emotions. It helps you move on.

Letting go is a choice. It can take some time, but when you get there you will feel lighter. Intentional action helps us bring about a mindset shift in order to let go. Keep in mind, you can't just let something go without there being some kind of validation. Again, you can do this for yourself. You don't need the offending party's participation in this process but you do need to acknowledge your experience. Processing your experiences through discussion, therapy, journaling and meditation will help you let go. Other ways to move through pain include writing letters to offenders, that you either send or burn, body work such as martial arts, yoga or running, even screaming can help shake things out of the body, and heal the mind and heart.

We seek validation to honor how an event has affected our lives. We have the right to want validation when we have been wronged, but we don't always get apologies. Many people who harm others don't care about the pain they cause. Stop begging for apologies from people who cause you harm. If they were good, kind people, they would not have harmed you. The apology you could get from someone like this, would not be sincere. Stop. Yes, it's hard to forgive someone when they haven't owned up to how they have affected you. Forcing forgiveness to try to forget a painful experience is disrespectful to yourself. Whether you are severing ties or adjusting expectations, think through whether forgiveness is even appropriate. You may decide that certain acts are beyond forgiveness, and that's okay. Sometimes, the road to healing includes setting a boundary that includes not forgiving what has been done to you or others. Some people refuse to forgive or accept apologies, as a safety net to remember the pain, therefore not allow that person into their lives again.

My Story

I was molested throughout my childhood by my stepfather. My mother admitted that she knew about it and did nothing. As horrible as this sounds it's uncomfortably common. My mind suppressed all those acts and betrayal for three decades. When the memories started to emerge in my late 30s, I was over-whelmed with rage. I talked to one of my closest friends about what I was remembering. My friend is a martial arts expert. I felt the need to protect myself even though there was no pre-sent threat to my safety. I think the present me was attempting to protect my inner child. I asked him what classes I should take to feel strong and tough. He said, "I think you should just punch the shit out of a boxing bag for a while". I admit I was a little disappointed. I wanted to learn either an elegant or lethal form of fighting to feel like Uma Thurman from the "Kill Bill" movies. He said I wasn't in any current danger so why "train" for something. He made sense. Training could have stoked feel-ings of hypervigilance. He felt I needed to get mad and get the old shit out of my mind and body. Training or learning some-thing new would have been another distraction. I found a kick-boxing gym near my house and signed up.

I attended my first class with girlfriends at a brand new gym in downtown Los Angeles. I didn't realize how much anger I'd been carrying, until I started hitting the bag. Quickly, tears rolled down my face. Every time I punched that bag I was fighting for the 6 year old me, too small to protect myself back then. I don't know how hard I cried, or for how long. I had no idea landing blow after blow, would unlock emotion that had been stored within me since I was a little girl. I don't remember walking home. I just remember hours later, being back in my apartment, wanting to call and apologize to the instructor and my friends, for making the class my therapy session.

Reflecting on my life, I'm sure I unleashed that pain on unde-serving friends, partners, co-worker, etc without even realiz-ing it. Hurt people hurt people. I needed to forgive myself for that. We carry so much of our pasts either on the surface, or deep within us. Looking back, I'm sure I lashed out, with reac-tions bigger than the present situation called for. Regardless of knowing if a reaction is for the present moment, or connected to something in our past we have to forgive ourselves and ask for forgiveness. It's not okay to use our trauma as an excuse for being assholes and acting immaturely. Having a huge reaction to a situation that isn't huge, means you've been triggered. Something in your current environment reminds you of *something* in your past – that *something* needs to be worked through and healed, so it's no longer a trigger. Your triggers are your responsibility, not others.

Forgiveness can go in multiple directions. It is extended to oth-ers for their transgressions towards us but we also need to for-give ourselves for how our actions affect others. We all have the ability to be the villain in someone else's life story. None of us is innocent all the time or beyond causing harm, and not everyone will forgive you. They have a right to handle situa-tions in their own way, in their own time. You can not be de-manding when asking for someone's forgiveness. You are not owed forgiveness. Just because you are ready for a situation to be resolved, does not mean the other person is on the same page. People are allowed to take their time to digest their feel-ings and decide if forgiveness, diving back into a relationship, or even a conversation with us is worth it for them. Sometimes it isn't and you need to accept that. Remember, you do not have to have a direct conversation with someone, to grow from the experience and move on.

Forgiveness isn't easy but it's worth it. It can help you accept the reality of a situation, yours and other people's limitations and boundaries. It can also help you move on from a space of perpetual disappointment, to peace. It's very complicated, and can be harder to do when you're constantly being wronged. Let's face it... some people just suck, and they're so far down in their rabbit hole of dysfunction, there's no getting out, no matter how much you love them. I put chronic drug users in this category. No one gets sober or changes their behavior, because someone else loves or prays for them to be healed. Addiction is a bitch, and managing severe mental illness is a hell of a mountain to climb. When someone manages to kick their addictions, or stick to a healthy mental health routine, they deserve a standing ovation but, you don't have to stand and clap, or let them back into your life.

You Don't Have To Forgive

Current sobriety or present good behavior, isn't an automatic pass for past behavior. No one knows how long their stability will last, so you have the right to protect yourself, and keep boundaries for as long as you need. Do what feels respectful and loving to yourself. You don't have to forgive. Or, you can choose to forgive and keep the offender at a distance. Just keep in mind, holding on to all the negative emotions connected with a person you haven't forgiven will weigh you down, not them. They will go on with their lives not caring how you feel. Forgiveness helps you.

Recently, a client spent a weekend reconnecting with family members that "vanished" in her teens when her father went to prison. She was justifiably angry that the people she loved the most all left when she needed them. She didn't know what to expect seeing them after so many years of silence. Being an adult with a child of her own, gave her the confidence to have tough conversations, and express feeling abandoned. She was surprised to learn that her family's decision to check out was their way of protecting themselves from her father's situation. Although she was a casualty of their decision, she understood their dilemma, and chose to shift her way of synthesizing the situation. She chose not to take their decisions personally. She'd spent years mourning their absence from her life, but due to her healing and skills on how to initiate tough conversations she was able to gain clarity, and offer forgiveness, that led to family reunification. She learned many valuable lessons, but the biggest was - When someone disappears from your life it may have nothing to do with you personally. They may not have the communication skills to articulate what's happening to them and walking away is the easiest option.

It took me a long time to understand that I needed to forgive my mother for allowing the abuse, but I didn't see the value in that for a very long time. Letting shit go is hard. It doesn't mean being hurt by someone doesn't matter. It doesn't mean you have to invite that person back into your life. It doesn't mean you've forgotten or plan to forget. It means the situation no longer has power over you, how you behave and how you live and love. To forgive is a way to honor your growth or kick start it. I'm not exactly sure when that process started between my mother and myself, but it definitely wasn't until I was in my 40s, more than ten years into my therapy. It's not something my therapist said I had to do. It was a gradual process and a choice I made on my own.

Recently, I participated in an ayahuasca ceremony and found myself crying out for my mother's forgiveness. I forgave her for not doing the things she didn't know were important to us. I forgave her for hurting us and allowing others to hurt us. I asked her to forgive me for all the negative things I've said about her over the years, knowing she had experienced her own traumas that weren't addressed, validated or healed. In all the preparation I did for the ayahuasca sit, I did not see this moment coming! I forgave my mother because she had to have gone through some horrible shit in order to inflict her own children with her unhealed pain. In my process, I also had to forgive my grandparents for whatever they did and didn't do to raise and protect her.

We need to forgive ourselves for how our behavior and thoughts harm us and others. Our actions can leave negativity lingering in our bodies in the form of negative self-talk, self-harm, addiction, etc. As Maya Angelou famously said, "Do the best you can until you know better. Then, when you know better, do better." Send love to the past versions of yourself that struggled to make good decisions. Send kindness to the versions of you that made decisions while in survival mode -

decisions that gave short-term pleasure or relief, but were harmful long-term. Send grace to the versions of you that didn't have guidance. If you are no longer doing all those things that caused harm to yourself or others, give thanks. You're growing.

Clients, new to therapy, often ask how they will know they are improving. Regularly, we have to deal with the same or similar situations over and over again. When you notice that you are handling these situations in healthier ways, by being more strategic, patient and less reactionary, you're healing.

CHAPTER 11
More Ways to Heal

In addition to the interventions included at the end of each chapter, there are more therapeutic modalities and methods you should know about. Some you can do on your own but some are best guided by a mental health professional. The following truths I will acknowledge: Therapy is not for everyone, and unfortunately isn't accessible by everyone. There are many great therapists out there but like chefs and mechanics - not all therapists know what they are doing. It's sad to say that some therapists can and do cause harm by either not knowing about helpful treatments that could bring about faster relief or initiating treatments that are out of their scope of practice. This is all the more reason to do your research on your therapist's training and ask questions. Never assume every therapist knows how to address every issue. It's not true and nearly impossible. Schools educate therapists by introducing us to many different theories from a variety of thought leaders, but there's so much material, it's hard for even the most prestigious schools not to skim over it. There are different therapeutic modalities and specific training is the financial and time responsibility of the therapist. Most training occurs post graduation, in the form of in-person or online training facilitated by other mental health professionals.

Doctors, lawyers and engineers and all therapists take personal time to receive specialized training in specific areas like autism, eating and personality disorders, trauma, couples counseling. If you need to heal trauma, it is extremely important you work with a therapist who has specific trauma skills and training. Don't assume that a therapist who treats anxiety / generalized anxiety disorder (GAD) has the training to treat Post Traumatic Stress Disorder or Acute Stress Disorder or Obsessive Compulsive Disorder. Although they all involve a level of anxiety they are not treated the same. An inexperienced therapist can unwittingly do harm to a client when they don't have the proper skill set to treat symptoms beyond their scope of practice. I've seen it attempted with bad results. Do your research and ask a ton of questions about a therapist's expertise and training. If you don't feel you and a potential therapist are a fit, say so, express your concerns and ask for referrals for other therapists. A confident therapist will not take this personally, and will usually give you referrals without you having to ask. Don't use the therapist calling you out and asking you to be present and honest, as an excuse to run from treatment. It's our job to present insights as we see it in order to deliver the proper interventions to help you heal. Sugarcoating your situation or dodging the obvious, so your feelings aren't hurt, is what your friends are for, not your therapist.

There are many different roads to healing. A methodology or technique that worked for a friend may not be appropriate for you, research and ask questions. I had a client who wanted to try Ketamine Therapy. I'd heard about it but didn't know much. She educated herself, enrolled in a program, and completed treatment with amazing results! Ketamine rewired her brain quickly, and was the perfect compliment to the talk therapy we were doing. I wish it had been discovered sooner. I wish I'd known more about it. I'm so glad she took that chance. Remember, you are the expert in your life. Your therapist is your co-pilot. Therapists aren't psychic. Therapists aren't your parents, and we don't know everything. Also, therapists do not tell you what to do. Therapists help you figure out who you are and guide you to get where you want to go. You make the decisions and changes. We offer interventions, insight and support. You are the driver or the brakes of your own healing. Therapists are your co-pilot until you want to fly solo again.

Below I listed several modalities, interventions and concepts that you should research to see if they may work for you or apply to you. This is in no way an exhaustive list, and this list does not equate to marching orders for what you should do next. Again, do your research and ask questions. There are many issues that require specialized treatment including eating disorders, chemical dependence, obsessive compulsive disorder, auditory and visual hallucinations, personality disorders, autism spectrum disorder and suicidal ideation. Again, this is not an exhaustive list. If you don't currently have a mental health professional in your life to consult with, start with your primary care physician or company EAP program. Many company EAP programs have licensed mental health professionals answering phones and handling the referral process.

It is important to share that some symptoms are too acute for once/weekly outpatient therapy. Do not diminish or ignore patterns of serious psychological distress. There are intensive outpatient programs (mental health treatment 2-3 times each week), partial hospitalization (treatment 5-7 days per week) or inpatient psychiatric treatment (24-hour crisis stabilization that lasts days or weeks) and medication. **Don't hesitate to call 911 or visit a hospital emergency department for an assessment or utilize a crisis line for resources BEFORE a situation becomes dangerous.** There are people trained to triage psychiatric distress. You don't have to do this on your own.

Therapeutic Treatments

Acceptance Commitment Therapy (ACT) - In the same family as Cognitive Behavioral Therapy but instead of trying to better control emotions, thoughts and behaviors, ACT teaches you to notice and 'sit with' difficult moments and embrace them. It utilizes mindfulness to accept your reaction to things and commit to make change.

Art Therapy is using artistic methods to treat psychological distress. The most common forms of art therapy are drama/theatrical, music (making & listening), visual (painting, drawing, photography), dance and writing. The goal is exploring and expressing emotions utilizing artistic methods to gain insight, and foster new coping strategies. Creating art can help you discover and accept how you feel. Art therapy can help decrease the symptoms of depression, anxiety and post traumatic stress disorder.

Attachment-Based Therapy - Attachment Theory was pioneered by John Bowlby, with further work completed by several other psychologists, including Mary Ainsworth. Work in this modality helps to address issues affecting relationships that stem from the varying levels of security and consistency experienced with early caregivers during childhood and infancy. The level of secure attachment in early childhood is directly correlated to your feelings of safety, security in later relationships.

Brainspotting is similar to Somatic Experiencing and EMDR (Eye Movement Desensitization Reprocessing) in that it focuses on the Mind-Body connection. It is a talk therapy technique used to treat trauma and utilizes where the eyes focus when a patient is feeling distressed or processing traumatic memories.

Cognitive Behavioral Therapy (CBT) - The most widely used and evidenced-based (backed by scientific study) therapeutic modality. It teaches the connection between our thoughts, feelings and behaviors. It's brief, highly effective and can help break unhelpful behavior patterns, that are driven by destructive thoughts and temporary feelings, within a few months.

Types of Couples Counseling

Discernment Couples Therapy is an assessment process that helps partners review their options when one partner wants to maintain a relationship when the other may want to end the relationship.

Emotion-Focused Therapy - A highly effective tool focused on the emotional state that helps identify destructive patterns that can damage attachment in relationships. EFT was developed by Dr. Sue Johnson and is most widely known as a modality in couples therapy. Very useful when one or both partners have PTSD or depression. It's under the Humanistic umbrella of therapy and relies on attachment theory as a base. It helps restructure distressed couple relationships into more secure connections.

Gottman Therapy is a research-based therapeutic model created by married couple Drs. Julie and John Gottman. The goal is to improve communication and intimacy and increase empathy. The Gottman method is very respected and many therapists invest in training due to its efficacy.

Imago Relational Therapy - Imago is latin for "image" and refers to the image of love that was implanted in childhood. It helps the individuals in a relationship look at the unmet needs experienced during childhood and how they play out in adult romantic relationships.

Narrative Therapy - The goal of all forms of narrative therapy is to separate the problem from the person IE Externalization. You are not the problem. The problem is the problem. This is very effective in couples therapy where one partner has the tendency to blame the other.

Solution Focused Therapy - This type of therapy is best utilized to tackle a specific issue, rather than managing a wide range of issues. Therapy starts with couples envisioning their ideal relationship, then working towards that goal.

Dialectical Behavioral Therapy (DBT)

DBT is also under the CBT umbrella and is broken into 3 modules: Mindfulness, Distress Tolerance, Interpersonal Effectiveness and Emotion Regulation. I included one skill from each module, but these BARELY scratch the surface. DBT is highly effective for people who tend to let their emotions dictate their actions, often recommended for people with bipolar and borderline personalities, disordered eating, have a history of self-harm, PTSD, those suffering with suicidal ideation, depression, anxiety and obsessive compulsive disorder.

A Mindfulness skill that is extremely simple, yet effective, is One Mindfully. This skill comes in handy when you feel overwhelmed by multiple tasks. Multitasking doesn't work. We spread ourselves thin trying to accomplish multiple things simultaneously, but usually end up taking too long to complete a few things poorly. One Mindfully suggests that you choose one thing to do and finish to completion without distraction. This can be difficult to imagine, but when incorporated in your daily life, can change how you handle everything for the better.

Non-Judgmental Stance is also a simple yet, when mastered, revolutionary skill. Do something, anything without judging it. For example - put on a dress without judging your body in it.

How about riding in a car and appreciating the view, solitude or ability to ride without the burden of driving. Instead of criticizing the seats, driver, age or model of car. Just ride. Now, incorporate that skill in a relationship situation.

Situation: Your partner loaded the dishwasher.

Judgmental Stance: Why did he put the glass on the bottom? He knows I hate when they start the machine in the morning.

Non-Judgmental Stance: I'm so glad I didn't have to do the dishes.

Distress Tolerance skills help you endure uncomfortable situations, without becoming overwhelmed or shutting down. You learn a combination of mindfulness, distraction and self-soothing techniques. Here's a Distress Tolerance skill you've probably been doing all of your life, making a Pros and Cons List to weigh your options when making decisions. Another useful and popular skill is TIPP (there are tons of acronyms in DBT) which stands for **T**emperature, **I**ntense Exercise, **P**aced Breathing, **P**rogressive Muscle Relaxation. This skill requires physical response to your body sensations. When we get upset our body temperatures rise. Splashing cold water on your face or holding an ice cube in your hand are helpful. Both will decrease your body temperature and shift your state of mind. Intense exercise can include sprinting down a hallway, driveway or jumping jacks - these things increase oxygen flow and can shake out anxiety, because you're exhausting yourself. Paced breathing is also something commonly done, but you probably didn't know it's a therapeutic skill. Boxed Breathing is a popular example that has you breathe in 4 second intervals: Inhale 4 seconds, hold 4 seconds, exhale 4 seconds and hold 4 seconds. Repeat until calm. PMR (progressive muscle relaxation) requires that you excessively lean into the tension your body is already feeling in order to relieve the tension. It's accomplished by tightening muscle groups one by one. You can start with your feet and move up to your face and head. Intensely squeeze each muscle group and hold for 5 seconds then release. You can say the words "squeeze" when tensing and "relax" when letting go. This skill helps to rid the body of stress and can even put you to sleep at night.

D.E.A.R.M.A.N (interpersonal effectiveness skill) – Sometimes scripting your part of a conversation, can help decrease any strong emotions that make it hard to have difficult conversations. You can also speculate how the other person will respond so you can feel more prepared. DEARMAN is a skill you can use when you need to ask someone to change something about their behavior. This skill is explained in Chapter 5 - Siblings.

Opposite Action (emotion regulation)– This method is as simple as it sounds. When faced with a difficult person, recall how you've reacted to them in the past. Now, when that person or situation comes back, do the exact opposite of what you normally do. If you ignore your mother's call. Why not pick it up and talk? Hear what's on her mind and disengage, when she crosses the boundaries you've set with her. If friends borrow money from you and never repay you – Stop and say no. Don't give them anything. They'll most likely move on and borrow from someone else.

Eye Movement Desensitization Reprocessing (EMDR) - One of the most effective trauma treatments worldwide involves moving your eyes side to side which helps process trauma. There is also a technique that involves a sound played in each ear. These movements stimulate the brain into reprogramming your reaction to your past traumas.

Emotion-Focused Therapy was developed by Dr. Les Greenberg to treat anxiety and trauma-related issues and symptoms. It focuses on your emotion responses.

Family Constellation - This method is not a traditional family therapy modality. Although this intervention focuses on repair, your family of origin is not directly involved in the session. You choose people within the group to act as stand ins for different family members, including yourself. A therapist acts as a facilitator and directs each person's position, posture, words and tone. They would intuitively act out family dynamics that need repair which is impossible due to death, distance or other reasons. It helps to ease the heart and mind in situations where otherwise there would be no resolution. This can also be accomplished in individual therapy utilizing a Sand Tray or Art therapy.

Family Therapy - The role of the family therapist is to facilitate conversations between family members that ignite change in negative patterns. Thus, members can create positive boundaries, improve intimacy and healthy communication. The major types of family therapy are Structural, Strategic and Transgenerational.

Structural Family Therapy can help a family get through divorce, other traumas as well as significant life transitions that will affect all the members. The family focuses on their interactions with each other and how negative behavior patterns create stress.

Transgenerational Family Therapy is exactly what it sounds like - managing conflict amongst multiple generations of your family. This treatment also helps when something traumatic has affected family members of multiple generations.

Strategic Family Therapy - This type of therapy is very helpful when there are adolescents with behavioral issues. Establishing a respectful hierarchy can help decrease familial distress.

Functional Family Therapy (FFT) - When kids are experiencing behavioral issues and have been referred for services, (CPS, juvenile courts, multiple inpatient hospitalizations due to be-havior, etc) FFT can be utilized at home, at school or in the community to bring stability to the family unit. Unfortunately the child acting out is usually labeled as the family problem, also known as The Identified Patient (description below) It is a strength-based short-term, yet intense practice that involves the entire family because the child that's expressing him or herself in negative ways, is not the only person experiencing distress within the family.

Gestalt Therapy - Focuses on present moments, not the past and sees the client as influenced by their current environment. Commonly used in the treatment of eating disorders.

Hypnotherapy - Clinicians use guided hypnosis to place pa-tients in a relaxed state, that allows them to focus on mental and physical health issues, in a less emotionally charged state.

Identified Patient - The "problem child" (although this person is any age) within a family, whose behavior is the personifica-tion of the entire family's dysfunction. Many families choose to single-out this person, place the blame of all the family prob-lems on their shoulders, try to get him/her treatment, all while ignoring the deeper issues that keep the family dysfunction go-ing. Very common in homes where a teen is acting out or abus-ing substances.

Internal Family Systems (IFS) - Unlike the name suggests, this modality is not a type of family therapy. This therapy works to access the self then heal the wounded parts of the self using the 8 Cs: calm, creativity, compassion, clarity, curiosity, connectedness and courage.

Inner Child Work - If you didn't feel loved, nurtured, accepted or protected consider doing therapy focusing on your inner child. You'll learn to re-parent yourself. All those judgmental things you feel and say about yourself can disappear. If therapy isn't your thing, no worries. Start with sitting alone for a while. Meditate on who you were as a kid. Write everything down. Did you have to take care of siblings, yet your own needs weren't met? Did you feel unsafe in your home or around certain people? Have you never heard the words "I love you" or "I'm proud of you?" from a parent? Validate those feelings of what you didn't get then – make it your mission to love, encourage and protect little you now. Be mindful of how you speak to yourself and correct or soften your verbiage when necessary. Usually our personal judgments are implanted in our childhood. If you mess up something, do not refer to yourself as "stupid" or "ridiculous" or anything negative. The world is tough enough, you don't need to punish yourself too. You are going to look at yourself as little you and say, "Little Michelle, you're safe now. Little David, you'll figure it out. Little Sarah, it's okay to ask for help." Unless you're an asshole, you would never shame, berate or abuse a child. You would support, provide love and protect a child, even a stranger. You deserve to be that kind and gentle with yourself too. Go play! Make cookies, take yourself camping or to an amusement park. Do all the things you missed out on, and reincorporate the things that brought you joy and relief in your childhood: camping, swimming, making cookies or reading. When I'm down or stressed I always go on a walk, preferably in nature or cook something. Usually both. It links me to my grandmother who was a phenomenal cook. I remember feeling safest at my grandparents' house. So when I need comfort I do the things that remind me of my most comfortable moments.

Jungian Therapy or Jungian Analysis - created by Carl Jung is a talk therapy that looks to integrate the conscious and subconscious parts of the mind, and analyze how past issues cause current psychological issues. Extroversion and Introversion theories originated with Carl Jung.

Motivational Interviewing - This is a client-centered technique used to gauge the stage of change a person is in, to change a negative behavior. There are four processes that include (in no particular order) evoking, engaging, focusing, and planning. This method is commonly used in substance abuse treatment.

Music Therapy - A trained professional utilizes music to elicit change. This is a very effective method with all populations, especially when working with the elderly. I've used this when working with resistant teen clients.

Neuro Linguistic Programming (NLP) - a series of techniques that rewire your brain in order to bring about desired outcomes. Can reduce anxiety, imposter syndrome and stress.

Psychoanalytic Therapy - Sigmund Frued was the creator of this method of talk therapy which focuses on the unconscious mind and bringing buried issues to the surface. Psychoanalysis encompasses the following concepts: transference, managing resistance and repression, dream analysis and word association.

Psychodynamic Therapy - based on work by Sigmund Freud helps the client work on their relationship with the outside world ie. relationships with others as opposed to the relationship between client and therapist. Works best with people who have the ability to be self-reflective.

Rational Emotive Behavior Therapy (REBT) - This method comes from Cognitive Behavioral Therapy/CBT. It helps to challenge unhelpful and erroneous thoughts that are rigid, irrational or unrealistic, and cause self-blame, which leads to behavioral and emotional disturbances.

Relational Therapy - A talk therapy (under the psychoanalytic umbrella) approach that posits healing relational issues, and maintaining healthy connections (utilizing courtesy, active listening, etc.) brings about improved self-esteem and well-being.

Sand Play Therapy - Highly effective with children who've experienced trauma, but sand play therapy can be useful with clients of all ages. It is a non-verbal technique that utilizes sand, toys and sometimes water to recreate a client's actions, thoughts and emotions, which are later reflected upon by the client and therapist.

Sand Tray Therapy - Sand is the conduit for discovery and healing. While working with sand in an imagined world, client's discover solutions to their problems with the guidance of a therapist.

Shadow Work Therapy - Originated by Carl Jung, this method is meant to help clients explore hidden or suppressed thoughts and feelings, in order to bring about deeper self-awareness to heal past traumas working with the unconscious mind to discover the parts of ourselves we hide. When you acknowledge and accept the dark sides of you it increases self-awareness and confidence. If you need to heal trauma you should do this with the guidance of a mental health professional.

Somatic Therapies - The goal of somatic therapies is to work on the body to bring about healing to the central nervous system. Extremely helpful when your physical body has been harmed.

Trauma Focused Cognitive Behavioral Therapy(TF-CBT) - Initially designed to help children heal from traumatic experiences. It's extremely effective, and has an easy to follow strategy to bring about relief from trauma symptoms. The skills learned will last a lifetime. (12-20 weekly therapy sessions with parental involvement).

Below you'll find ways to heal without relying on an outside source. This is not an exhaustive list by any means, and I feel it's best to work with a licensed professional to help you reflect and learn how to move forward positively.

Validation and Normalization – I believe validation and normalization are effective tools all healthy people utilize regularly. It diminishes feelings of shame and loneliness, when you realize you're not the only person to go through your situation. Also, how much better do we feel, when we share our thoughts and feelings with someone, and they understand us. You can do that for yourself. You can learn to trust yourself.

FOO (Family of Origin) – Exploring your childhood, and the caregivers who influenced who you are and how you see the world, is crucial to understanding how you make decisions, and how you feel about yourself.

Genogram – I'm a big fan of using genograms to trace the patterns of your family of origin. It looks like a family tree, but instead of stopping at who married who and conceived specific kids, it tracks relationship patterns. Which family clusters dealt with substance abuse or domestic violence. Are there multiple marriages and/or divorces? Who initiated these acts? It helps you acknowledge the past so you can heal the present, and prepare for the future. When I completed a genogram of my family I discovered a pattern of motherly abandonment and sibling rescues. Multiple aunts took over the raising of their sister's children. Myself and my little sister included. When you see patterns like this, it can help explain why decisions were made and how the groundwork was laid to perpetuate certain patterns. This helps lessen any shame you could feel internalizing behaviors that are in your DNA.

Exposure Therapy /In Vivo Therapy is a brief therapy that works by slowly, gradually and strategically exposing one to the thing that stokes fear. This guided exposure builds distress tolerance, therefore, decreasing anxiety. Situations that can be helped by exposure therapy include public speaking, being in crowds, etc. I utilized this therapy to help a teen client who witnessed a mass shooting at her school.

Mindfulness - This type of therapy teaches the client to be more present and aware of emotions and thoughts in order to decrease automatic maladaptive reactions.

Radical Acceptance - Is a concept that will set your heart free, once you've mastered it. It's more challenging than it sounds, so be patient with yourself and give yourself time. You'll know you've mastered Radical Acceptance, when the person or situation that usually irritates you, doesn't. You're able to shrug instead of engage.

Writing Letters - Writing letters is extremely powerful, because the activity helps you process on multiple levels. Writing helps us engage our logical mind, which creates space between ourselves and our emotions, and allows us to gain perspective. You can write a letter whether you plan to send it or not. The act of getting your thoughts out of your head, and assigning feelings, helps to process by making you articulate them for someone else to understand. It helps you grasp the situation first. I'm a big fan of writing down what's on your mind because it can be helpful to get clear about your thoughts and possibly script important points to make during difficult conversations, that can make you too emotional to effectively engage.

Journaling – Writing about your experiences has been a practice for writers for centuries. I believe the act has lasted so long is because it's effective. Some get intimidated by a blank page, but free yourself from any pressure of the outcome. Journaling is not a formal endeavor. You are not turning it into a teacher (or therapist) to grade. You don't have to share it with anyone. You don't have to consider grammar or spelling. Just write and release. Always keep a journal or notebook with you so you can jot down ideas, epiphanies throughout your day. Yes, there are apps that do this now but writing with a pen or pencil triggers an emotional part of the brain that technology can't activate in the same way. That's why so many people still prefer flipping pages in a book. You could write just before going to bed, because it can help clear the mind before sleeping. If writing free-style isn't your thing, it's very easy to locate journals that have daily prompts that can get you going.

Attachment Work: Diving into attachment work can be very rewarding because it answers so many questions about how you engage in relationships. Doing this work can help you heal your Insecure, Avoidant or Disorganized attachments, and learn how to feel more open and trusting, in order to engage securely in healthy relationships. It's also helpful in analyzing the attachment styles of the people you've been attracted to in the past, to understand what contributed to the dysfunction of those relationships.

Steps to Heal Attachment Wounds

*"Our brains continually form maps of the world – maps of
what is safe and what is dangerous."*
- Dr. Bessel van der Kolk

Complex or Relational Trauma can arise from prolonged peri-
ods of aversive stress, usually involving entrapment (psychological or physical), repeated violations of boundaries, betrayal, rejection and confusion, marked by a lack of control and
helplessness. Common situations include being bullied, har-
assment, physical, sexual and emotional/verbal abuse, domestic violence and substance abuse, stalking, threats, separation
and loss, unresolved grief and neglect (Doctor, R., 2017).

1. Acknowledge the loss of what could have been. Denial
   is not helpful. If you deny your pain, you delay your
   healing.

2. Acknowledge your feelings - Linda felt horrible that
   parenting her child was such a struggle. Even harder
   was admitting all the anger, exhaustion and defeat she
   felt doing the job we're told women should be able to do
   perfectly, and with ease. The best thing you can do is allow yourself to feel. If a situation has rocked your world,
   why act like it hasn't?

3. Acknowledge the conflict caused by your relational
   wounds. Can you see negative patterns in your work
   life, romantic history? If you've experienced frequent
   relational distress in all areas of your life, the common
   denominator is you. Everything can't always be someone else's fault.

4. If your life is consistently chaotic, acknowledge this
   then track your contributions to your chaos.

Incorporate new coping strategies to manage your dysfunctional patterns.

5. Improve coping and communication skills to improve confidence and self-worth in relationships.

Dealing with Highly Manipulative People

Toxic and manipulative people are challenging to say the very least. You could choose to cut them out of your life or avoid them completely, but you can't control if they come into your world in a capacity you can't control like being a neighbor, co-worker, boss or parent. It's best to learn ways to manage yourself and the interactions. Here are a few ways to interact without getting sucked into their self-centeredness:

1. Limit your engagement - set specific start and end times to interact.

2. Do not offer extensive explanations to justify your decisions. For example, "Dad, yes, I can meet you for lunch but only if it's on Thursday at 12:30. We need to finish lunch by 1:30pm. If you can agree to that, I'll make a reservation."

3. Don't ask questions. If you must ask questions, don't ask follow-up questions.

4. Be direct. Don't expect a manipulative to person to take hints or read between the lines.

Gray Rocking

Dysfunctional attention seekers need their egos constantly fed and they never get full. Another way to limit your interactions with a manipulator is by Gray Rocking which basically means - be boring. When you have to communicate with a manipulator, if possible, deliver only one-word responses to their questions. Never ask open-ended questions. These people tend to weave stories to elicit attention. If their stories aren't complete lies they are usually embellished. Dull your expressions to be unappealing. Your goal is not giving the toxic person any information to latch onto. If they start to tantrum, avoid eye contact and remove yourself from the situation. Don't get amped up with them. Don't attempt to solve their problems. They will move on when they realize they don't have an audience. Let them fly their toxic plane solo, without you as a co-pilot.

Don't challenge a narcissist or manipulative person. They'll never back down and want to have the last word. If you have truth on your side there's no need for you to defend it. Let them hold onto their warped thinking, they'll never submit, so why fight? You can try these words, "We remember things differently" or "That wasn't my experience." Why try to defend your stance with a defense offender? Their goal will never be taking accountability. Their goal is to be right. You can't reason with a toxic person. You can't convince them of anything that they don't want to understand. They have low self-worth and major insecurities disguised behind huge egos and, in many instances, large success. They don't see you, therefore, they don't care how you feel. Nothing you can do will change that. They are reactive and always feel as if they're being attacked. They are both victims and bullies. Don't try to reason with them. Save yourself and walk away.

What if you have to maintain contact with one of these people, because they are the spouse of a loved one, co-worker, boss, neighbor, etc. Be undesirable. Decline all invitations. Remember, be boring. Excuse yourself from conversations and events. If you don't feel confident yet and don't know how to manage the situation, lie if you have to. For example, "I wish I could attend your party but I have a cold. I have plans already. I can't find a babysitter. I'm married. I'm asexual and don't date. I'm going out of town." Yes, honesty is the best policy but some people live in fantasy lands of their own design and have no room for your truth. Also, many of these people are stupid, violent and don't care about consequences. You could be in danger if you innocently engage with one of them honestly. Many people have been sexually assaulted by people who felt they were being challenged simply by declining a date.

If you want to engage, feel safe and don't shut down easily - go for it by being honest. Put on your armor and get ready for battle. "I'm not attending your event because that's not my vibe." "I won't babysit your kids because they don't behave well." "I won't date you because I don't feel respected in your presence." I'm not hosting the family reunion because you never help in any way." Here are a few things I've told people in the past. "We aren't friends because we are very different people." "Let's be honest, we really don't like each other. I'm okay with that. You can be too" "I don't respect the choices you make. Our lives arc very different."

Some people don't like 'burning bridges' but I say FLAME ON! When you know there's a difference in values, there's no mutual respect and you have no desire to have someone in your life, why not be honest? The best that could happen is the person takes your honesty and uses it as a catalyst for their evolution. Keep expectations low though. People don't change unless they want to. People who conduct themselves in manipulative and destructive ways are usually too emotionally immature to allow for honesty with themselves or others. Growth requires vulnerability and vulnerability requires honesty.

Saying Goodbye - Sometimes relationships fade away or abruptly end without the opportunity to say our peace, and move on. Sometimes we have the opportunity to tell someone why we're walking away. If that is your plan, talking about it with your loved one could help the other person not feel abandoned. Having a direct conversation could also help decrease the chance the person doesn't cast themselves as the victim, by creating their own narrative about the events. This isn't something you have to do. It's okay to be misunderstood, especially by a toxic person. If you decide to dive in, start the conversation with facts, not your emotions. Describe the dynamic you've had and all the reasons you need to walk away. Your decision doesn't have to make sense to the other person. Don't feel like you need to convince them why you're walking away. You are not asking for their permission. If you decide to love someone from a distance you can add, "I love you, but our relationship cannot continue." It may soothe the blow for you and the other party.

Honor a situation that can no longer be. I'm a big fan of making lists. A list can be your evidence of the situation, which validates how you feel, and the reasons why you're making this decision. It can also show the other party how often they've harmed you, if you've never mentioned your grievances previously. When you need to mourn a person or situation, try making a list of all that you learned, skills acquired, insights, experiences and gifts attained. Honoring the situation for what it gave you, reframes the relationship and balances out the negativity with some positivity. Time is never wasted. You have the choice to see the positive in every scenario and, therefore, thank the person or experience for what it has given you.

How to get to a place to allow yourself to let it go: We can only truly mourn when we're in a place of acceptance. You can only live authentically if you're standing in truth. Remember Radical Acceptance? Owning, acknowledging and accepting the situation for what it was. Be really honest with yourself about your situation, not languishing in the 'potential'. Betting on someone's potential is a lose-lose situation. Your expectations of someone's potential mean nothing. Your ideas of what someone could or should be or do isn't helpful, especially if those dreams aren't mutual. People have their own dreams, desires and can own their capabilities or lack thereof. Hinging your future dreams on someone else's potential is a huge waste of your time. You'll start by being angry at the other person then eventually become angry with yourself later. Be honest. Own your situation, relationship or the truth of the other person, so you can shift into the mode you need to be in to serve yourself. You can't get help or heal when you are in denial. Also, maintaining expressed or unexpressed expectations for another person is toxic. Your idea of someone else's potential can be disrespectful, distressing, demeaning and exhausting. In Susan Anderson's book, "Taming the Outer Child" she speaks to the denial some choose in order to keep their heads in the sand. "Many people prefer to stay in denial rather than accept the givens in their situation. They try to change the unchangeable. Protesting reality only squanders precious time and energy. Railing against the unchangeable is just spinning your wheels - you don't gain any traction."

If you're reading this book you're most likely a grown up, so act like it. Stop acting like bad things don't happen to good people. We grow the most from the rough stuff we experience. Instead of judging yourself for past decisions, you need to forgive yourself and others and lean into loving yourself, which means accepting yourself, warts and all.

Although experiencing loss is an inevitable part of life, there are ways to help cope with the pain, come to terms with your grief, and eventually, find a way to pick up the pieces and move on with your life. Here are some steps to consider

1. Acknowledge your pain.
2. Accept that grief can trigger many different and unexpected emotions.
3. Understand that your grieving process will be unique to you.
4. Seek out face-to-face support from people who care about you.
5. Support yourself emotionally by taking care of yourself physically.
6. Recognize the difference between grief and depression. Both can be temporary or lifelong.

If you find yourself questioning your judgment, intelligence, skill or grit, make a list of all that you know for sure about yourself. Lean into the facts about your life, character, identity, not other's opinions or your own fears. Listing these things helps remind you of all you've accomplished and survived, and help you build confidence to get through tough situations, conversations, and relationships. I wrote my list several years ago and refer to it whenever I'm experiencing a low moment. Here it is:

I can handle hard situations. I've moved to major cities alone and created great relationships and lucrative careers.

Despite growing up severely shy I had the courage to do comedy for several years in front of crowds of strangers even when I was scared. I learned that my voice matters.

I had the courage to go back to school at 39 years old to help people feel better. I studied a completely new field and earned a masters degree in clinical psychology.

I am loved. I have wonderful friends and family that listen, support and help me when I need them. I'm grateful I've been accepted into the lives of so many wonderful people.

I survived years of childhood abuse and chaos. I can survive anything that comes my way.

I have jumped out of an airplane, been parasailing, scuba dived and swam in the open ocean where there wasn't a bottom to touch or side for me to grab onto.

Even though I was taught to keep my pain to myself, I am now strong enough to ask for help when I need it. I'm grateful I always receive it.

I was hired to host a children's show with no prior television experience. I trusted the talent someone else saw in me even if I didn't see it in myself.

I trust my ability to make good decisions even when I'm scared. I know that I can change my mind when I need to and still be okay.

I have traveled around the world alone. Even when I'm nervous and scared I know I will eventually get where I need to go even if I don't know the language. I'm very resourceful.

As you're processing these moments, also include lessons you're happy you learned, skills you've acquired and adventures in which you've participated. Reframing situations in your favor and a healthy dose of hope can set the stage for living a more authentic life with confidence. You can thrive despite your setbacks.

LET'S STAY CONNECTED

Follow me on Instagram at: MelodyLMFT,

Find me at:
www.MelodyLMFT.com

Join the conversation at:

Mourning The Living on Facebook

Additional Press Release and other Author Related
Information Available at:

www.MelodyInspires.com

RESOURCES & ACKNOWLEDGEMENTS

This book could not have been written without the trust of my clients, friends and family. I would also like to acknowledge the many therapists, psychologists, psychiatrists and authors whose work contributed to the success of this book.

- "Adult Children of Emotionally Immature Parents" by Dr. Lindsay Gibson

- "Attached" and Amir Levine and Rachel Heller

- "It Didn't Start With You" by Mark Wolynn

- "The Drama of the Gifted Child" by Alice Miller

- "David and Goliath" by Malcom Gladwell

- "Healing Relational Trauma with Attachment-Focused Interventions: Dyadic Developmental Psychotherapy with Children and Families" by Dan Hughes

- "Homegoing" by Yaa Gyasi

- "Understanding your Grief: Ten Touchstones for Finding Hope and Healing Your Heart" by Dr. Alan Wolfelt

- "The Book You Wish You Parents Had Read by Phillipa Perry

- "Taming Your Outer Child" by Susan Anderson

- "The Art of Extreme Self Care" by Cheryl Richardson

- "Post Traumatic Slavery Syndrome" Dr. Joy DeGruy

- "My Grandmother's Hands"

- "The Deepest Well" by Dr. Nadine Burke Harris

- Self-Esteem by McKay and Fanning

- "Shadow Work Journal and Workbook for Beginners: An Easy to Follow Guide to Develop Self-Awareness and Find Your True Self With Many Journal Prompts and Exercises (The Power of Healing)" by Cher Hampton

- "Taming the Outer Child" by Susan Anderson

- Non-Violent Communication: A Language of Life by Marshall B. Rosenberg

- "Waking the Tiger" by Peter Levine

- "When our Grown Kids Disappoint Us."

- "Your Brain on Food"

www.ingramcontent.com/pod-product-compliance
Lightning Source LLC
Chambersburg PA
CBHW052123270326
41930CB00012B/2742